BOOKS BY PETER VIERECK

I. POETRY:

Terror and Decorum. Charles Scribner's Sons, New York, 1948.
Pulitzer Prize, 1949.

Strike Through the Mask! Scribner's, 1950.

The First Morning. Scribner's, 1952.

The Persimmon Tree. Scribner's, 1956.

II. PROSE:

Metapolitics: From the Romantics to Hitler. Alfred A. Knopf, New
York. (Swedish edition, 1942; Italian edition, 1948.)

Conservatism Revisited: The Revolt Against Revolt. Scribner's,
1949.

*Shame and Glory of the Intellectuals: Babbitt Jr. vs. the Redis-
covery of Values*. The Beacon Press, Boston, 1953.

*Dream and Responsibility: Four Test Cases of the Tension Between
Poetry and Society*. The University Press of Washington, D.C.,
1953.

The Unadjusted Man, A New Hero for Americans. Beacon Press,
Boston, 1956.

Conservatism: From John Adams to Churchill. Anvil paperback,
Van Nostrand Co., Princeton, New Jersey, 1956.

Metapolitics: The Roots of the Nazi Mind. Capricorn pocketbook,
G. P. Putnam's Sons, New York, 1961.

III. VERSE DRAMA:

The Tree Witch. Scribner's, New York, 1961.

THE TREE WITCH

THE
TREE
WITCH

a poem and play

(first of all a poem)

by PETER VIERECK

Charles Scribner's Sons, NEW YORK

ACKNOWLEDGMENT TO PERIODICALS

Excerpts from this book have appeared in:

Approach, Audience, Chelsea Review, Contact, Epoch, Four Quarters,
Harper's Magazine, Harvard Advocate, Inland, The Literary Review,
New Mexico Quarterly, The New Republic, New York Herald-Tribune,
Noonday, Northwest Review, The Paper (Chicago), Poetry (Chicago),
The Prairie Schooner, Saturday Review, The Second Coming, University
of Houston Forum.

Though it is not customary to acknowledge the kindness of one's own
publisher, the painstaking effort undergone by Scribner's in preparing
this book was so generous and so considerable that the author wishes
to record his particularly grateful recognition.

PRINTED IN THE UNITED STATES OF AMERICA

Library of Congress Catalog Card Number 61-7221

TO ANYA

CONTENTS

DRAMATIS PERSONAE, STAGING, ETC.

First professional performance: May 31–June 3, 1961 by the Poets' Theater of Cambridge, Mass., in Harvard's new Loeb Drama Center. (1961 readings of major excerpts: Johns Hopkins Poetry Festival; Harvard-Radcliffe Festival of the Arts at Quincy House.)

Written during 1955–60, this book may be read either as poem or verse-play, stage aspects being clearly bracketed apart from the poetry to minimize their intrusion. Each of the numbered scene-titles—call them chapter-titles if read as poem only—indicates a lapse of time and change of topic but not necessarily a change of setting. Preliminaries (list of personae, costumes, etc.) follow.

1. (*Dramatis personae and costumes.*)

The three voices of the poem—the adjusted moderns, the aunts, and the Hellenic dryad—are identified as WE, THEY, and SHE in left-hand margin. Group speeches, WE or THEY, are spoken not collectively but by individual actors, taking turns as group-spokesman wherever suitable. Indented lines suggest a mood-change when read as a poem; a voice-change when acted as play; also a change of group-spokesman when in WE or THEY speeches.

The guardian aunts, three in number, are got up as a business-woman, a Helen Hokinson club woman, and a white-smocked lab director; all beam with success and benign sincerity. Looking simultaneously middle-aged and schoolboy, the "we" are tailored with business suits above the waist, boyscout shorts below. Since the varying we-spokesmen are expressing varied levels of the same modernity (intended to differ also in levels of sophistication and diction), their additional details of costuming may be varied accordingly; so may their number. When impersonating others in the vaudeville scene, the dryad wears temporarily the gaudy costumes the text specifies. But when in her own role, her appearance (Greek tunic) and her manner (esp. in her crucial songs) have to be two things: plain and casual. An honest staging of her shall avoid both the charm-claptrap of glamor and the soulful gauzy-gownsy trappings of quainte poesie. Avoid at all cost—in staging, acting, costuming, and enunciation—the romantic Hellenizing of the late

19th century; cf. the dryad's Athena speech in scene 6,

> Yet what's less Greek than pedant posing pagan?
> To find us excavate yourself, not Greece.
> In your own skull, nine egos deep, lies Troy.

2. (*Problem of Staging Magic.*)

All mystery of possibly non-material implications (esp. the ter-
rorizing hint of the real Aphrodite on page 78 and of the claws on
page 97) should be so staged and acted as to hover between
material and magical explanations, never resolved. That is, never
wooing an audience with the demagogy of a "solution," the convenience of a system. The latter convenience—the dehydrating
compulsion to classify (whether scientifically or religiously) the
untidy tides of our being—is less to the present purpose than the
tides themselves.[1] Nor need the stage director make concessions
to realism, or other isms; at times the sensuous connotations of
lyric fantasy may be closer to reality—even to social reality—than
the systematized denotations of either objective social photography
or didactic social ideology. Indeed that same contrast—between
an embodied rhythm of life and an abstracted philosophy of life—
is the "dramatic conflict" not merely of these pages but of reality
all around us. Hence Maggie's "I don't much like humanity; / My
love is lilt, not vow" (p. 47).

Thereby the familiar 2-cornered fight of materialism vs. current
"religion" (equally cliché on both sides) becomes 3-cornered;
the dryad is the unfamiliar third. Corners 1 and 2 are the cold
geometries of utility and religiosity; their signs are metallic and
galactic blueprints respectively. Corner 3 consists of "the gods"
—that is, the warm spontaneities—of leaf, lilt, love; their signs

---

[1] The words "tides" and "growth" are used in this book in the sense of
Boris Pasternak's affirmation that "life is never a material, a substance to
be molded . . . life is the principle of self-renewal . . . transfiguring
itself;" in that sense a growing tree is nothing passive. It is a dramatic
act, a dryad gesture; through root and leaf it unifies earthiness and
airiness, mortality and sky, in concrete touchable simplicity. Wonderfully
impure and mixed-up, this here-and-now small-and-local simplicity eludes
the grandeurs of either machinery or spirituality, the former too busybody,
the latter too cosmic, and both too Procrustean as solvers, saviors, naggers
of the world.

are season, cycle, circle (as opposed to straight-line mechanical progress); these spontaneities are not the formless, diffuse impulse known as romanticism but are compressed into classic form through inner organic growth (the "wild sap, strict dance" of p. 110, the "strict quicksilver" of p. 28, the "core" of p. 58 with its "repose of flight"). Corner 1 (hedonist materialism) is subnatural; corner 2 (joyless respectable "religion") is supernatural; corner 3 is neither and both, being magical but a natural magic, the marriage of earth and sky, giving birth to the now-exiled sisterhood of dryad and Aphrodite. In the contrasting lyric rhythms and contrasting images of the theme-setting third autumn song, corners 1 and 2 ("godless joy and joyless God") are both overcome by the dryad of the autumn wine-god festival ("the gods who are dishevelment of God"). This particular conflict is better expressed in verse-drama than in prose-drama because its universal inarticulate emotions can be felt sensuously through conflicting rhythms or images rather than spelt out explicitly through either intellectual repartee or bang-bang physical blows.

3. (*Reconciling the lyrical and the dramatic.*)

And where there is dramatic conflict, poem overlaps with play in genre. The distinction between lyric mood and action mood in life—between perused *verse*-play and performed verse-*play* in letters—is overcome during those intensities when imaginative inwardness is projected onto outer conflicts. When involving us deep enough, songs are not merely about actions; songs *are* actions. In the end [2] the only ones.

[2] In stages. "In the beginning," words tell us, was the word; not the event (events are pseudo-actions); and not yet the true action of song (song is word-in-depth, the word as undertow). In a kind of middle period comes the thing called "events," a surface ripple of headlines and statistics. In the end all shall be song.

ACT I

Scene 1, TRAPT AND SPITTING

[We stand reminiscing before unraised curtain, perhaps as if reply-
ing to questioning manner of late-arrivals among us on stage or
among audience below. Placard on curtain: "Abortive PRO-
LOGUE."]

WE: Callously innocent in our disinfected games,
We plastic-swaddled children of fifty years
With unlined faces, hacking down some gnarls,
Unpeeled a dryad once, stript, trapt, and spitting,—
That older race, filth of unswaddled pulse-beat,
A god and shieldless, uninnocently tender.
        We marched right back, yanking a god we cornered:
        A lassoed cataract amid canals.
First visit there let's kiddingly recall,
The hours of swapping new toys for old spells,
Till
[bowing toward entering aunts]
    sobered by the hygiene-spraying aunts.

[Aunts, while entering, cut short our reminiscing PROLOGUE by
raising up curtain on the play itself. For this and later scenes basic
setting is yard in front of open-doored garage, with garage floor-
space occupied not by car but straw bedding.]

THEY: What makes our young ones fuss round just some
        stump?
Go clutter honest lumber up with spooks,
Read dryads in, go hunt for haunters; yet
When all is said and done of myth and magic,
One flashlight shrivels any hunk of dusk.
[They aim at straw bedding with flashlights and DDT.]
        But watch for tricks: with lyric buzz re-enter
        Flies, incense, backwardness,—those Old Expelled.

WE: Her spells?

THEY: Her frauds! Aim lights—look, nothing there.

WE: Frauds of the dryad: speech, growth, weapon mock us.
Her weapon: raids by quicksilver evadings.
Her growth: a land tide, disrespectful as
Leaves stretching their first fingers. Her speech:
Gust of alleys, a truant from sidewalks and systems,
Leaving behind a litter of petals and doubts.

THEY: There was the time she seemed to wrench your veins
         loose.

WE: Of anti-metal something shimmered then
(A winging of sap against a steeling of will)
That would have rusted something of machine in us,
Had something in us of weight not tamed that wine.

THEY: Tame gods by gifts.
Give metal's just-as-good.
Proclaim: "Instead! Instead!"
She needs; you give; she changes.
And so a god gets nursed into a pet;—

WE: But threshes about. Exchanged her tree-home—
Imagine being cooped in living coarseness!—
For kind soft straw we dumped upon the pavement
Of this prefab garage we lavished on her,
A half-mile from our street. Ingratitude
Of gods we house! Not one gift works
To stop that twisting on that first-class straw.

THEY: With soundproof walls we've safely sealed you from
         her.

WE: Into our sleep a far-off tossing rustles;
A twirl of arms and leaves; recurrent dream:—

FEMININE VOICE [*off-stage*]:
No start,
  Around around,
    She is a god she is a plant
      Undertow of flesh and ocean
      Ocean and flesh of undertow
    A plant is she a god is she
  Around around,
No end.

WE [*pointing where dream-voice came from*]:
That obscene vibrance jars our own snug beds
And blights new cribs from birth with undertow.
Dear aunts, we have bad dreams, seal unrest out.

THEY: So much of other nuisance, junk, and murk
We've killed for its own good, to scrape earth pure;
But when some bitch-dog wags immortal hide,
Our "put her out out of her misery" won't put.

WE: What cannot kill unkillable can torture;—

THEY: She, writhing stubborn, jars us even more.

WE: A rotten gyp when gift and gun both fail;
No other vermin lasts; it's them, it's she, it's
Immortals always spoil our cleaning up.

THEY [*to each other*]:
And so a pet gets cursed into a god.

.   .   .

WE: Next dream, half farce: she sowed—amid tame starches—
Song's fleeing laurel (wiggly still with nymph)
And love's wild myrtle;
                                now a crop of sighs
Drowns out the crackle of our breakfast cornflakes.
Spry aunts, help quick; growth shrinks us; school in panic.
Whatever sprouts, throbs to the dryad's tossing.

THEY: Growth just won't shape like plastics, you poor boys;
To wither myrtle, plant it in a pot;
To wither laurel, spray it with a footnote.
But darker than her wars, her lures. Those fancy
God-molls got gossiped of in Arcady.
Neighbors saw them bend near bulls, and as for swans—.
Then stomp more moral than a quadruped;
Be well-scrubbed knights; in short,
                                go lynch that foreigner.
[*to each other:*]
And so reversed creation ousts a god.
From deicide, man deified. But she—

SHE [*entering suddenly*]:
What hoists mirage can't push one jonquil up.

THEY [*pointing at her indignantly*]:
The outcast calls our miracles mirages.
We call her skirts and petals camouflages.
The roots of flowers smuggle earthquakes up.
All beauty is a whiff of the abyss.

SHE: Bloom is serene explosion.

THEY: We'd rather build.

WE: Build, build! Climb higher, higher.

THEY: Stems of girders
Are made, not bloomed. Made without skirts or petals
[*ripping flowers from her waist*]
Flouncing a rainbow-ring around an ambush.

WE: Gray steel climbs mushroom-straight.

SHE: Spore, shammed from sand, climbs facile,
                                        towers, keels.

THEY and WE [*as if chorusing tribal war-cry*]:
We master matter, make it jump through hoops.

SHE: O slogan me no Atlas from your engines.
Weight lifts but weight, the globe or any feather.
Meanwhile the heart ebbs. Only heart lifts heart.

THEY: That last hold-out (ebb of grove and wave) we'd
Crunch,
          could we crack just once its rhythm. We can't.
[*Aunts leave.*]

SHE: Castaways hoard the annals of beginnings,
The alphabets of dawn before the split.
Two signs, when first your campfire banned us, wrangled:
Circle and line. Our cycle, your ascent.
"Revere each season's own true swerve," we sang then;
"Drain, build, stamp logic on," clanged will, male, steel.
Clang-knit geometries of girders garland
Your plumb-lines now
                         and grid our zigzag ways.

WE: Hail man-the-improver,
For his is the world without end. In techniculture
A few inventions more, then all wilds harnessed;
Weeds, gods hacked out by will, by male, by steel.

Bulldozer world: grove's awe and rubble razed for
A smile of blueprints on a surge of chins.

SHE: Your lavishness with clicks and slot-machines—

WE: —(here tin gives birth, true stainless birth, not life's
  kind)—

SHE: —is but man's fear of liking being owned again
By cornucopian lap—

WE: —all nest and trap and
Prayer lips and infinite pillowing mercy and quicksand.

SHE: Girl was the older race's core, unshrined by
Who shrines machine, the heavy public man
Too willed to play or pray. And girlhood once
Uprooted roots out child, man, landmark too,
Untending
              —to be priestess means to tend—
The linking ivy of a heritage.
Apart, apart the mute shared sap-flow dries,
Into a crackle of unclutching. Hail
The chattery scorch-torch-ping of progress popping.

WE: We hustle off the landmarks to the archives.
We've freed you, freed you all, from all of that.
Stop priestess-ing around in moth-chawed wardrobes;
What's left to "tend" but singsong-rusted lute-strings?
Our rust-proof nerves twang prose.

SHE: What have you prosed us to?—once tide, ode, bud.
Good for your files and glands, the thing your time-clock
And cot call "woman" means but gelded male.
Yet girl-lap templed—inner Delphi—teaches

Doer what grower knows of spell and rite,
Willing what being knows of soul and gut.

WE: A belly swelled into an oracle?
Let earth be earth, let womb be just plain womb
(Not peep-hole into Earth-in-capitals),
And each one plowed by reasoned appetite.

SHE: Don't think apart the mixed-up dark of things.
As we need your half, starving you'll need ours;
No crop from conquering will, without our magic.
Spray all your fruit-trees clean, they still won't dangle
Till fouled into life by dryad-rut within.

  . . .

[*Long silence of mutual non-comprehension. Hesitantly she kisses
we-spokesman, as if assessing him, then shivers disappointedly and
strikes his cheek with back of hand. Does same to rest of us in
turn. We stumble around in rage, hunting for her; vainly hunting,
because she freezes into tree-imitation, drooping her arms like
branches, a rope in one, fruit in other. Phrases that follow alternate between us, as indicated by line-breaks.*]

WE: Stop her, catch her.
     She's over there.
        No, there!
You'd almost think we've slap-inviting faces.
Sheer evil; give her jail.
     No, shock treatment;
She's mad.
   No, evil.
     No, mad *and* evil.
        Nothing
Here but a fruit-tree.
    No, a gallows tree.

But look, that's plainly a plum. Is it for us?
No, that's a rope. Is it for us? I'm thinking
[*voice grows gentle*]
We all must hang ourselves [*puts head in noose*].
[*another grabs fruit and roars:*] No, eat, eat, eat!

[*Aunts march in, aiming flashlight at her; she flees into garage.*]

THEY: A lesson: stay awake near gods. No fruit tree,
No rope was there. Only the dregs stirred up
From your own sleep. She has no life, no power
Except through your free choosing.
[*low voice:*]   **Nor do we.**

WE-SPOKESMAN:
I used to think that only windbags waddled
In prophet robes. But now my nerve-strings,
Splicing with her straw, are rustling forth the future;
Future on tiptoe waits my cue.

THEY [*in whisper to each other*]:
The secret Concordat!—don't let him guess it.
Our secret history among the old ones.

WE-SPOKESMAN:
In us, in them, in her—by chance? by plan?—
Eons collide. Big unknown eons (fathomed
By us no more than floods by flotsam) balance
On how our smallness outmaneuvers hers.

      .   .   .

These words I said just now: my own? my own?
Or echoes from her rustling on the floor?
Who absorbs whom?

THEY: You her. By six maneuvers.
[*counting off each number pedantically on fingers; classroom-voice*]
First, humble her: an exhibit for tourists to finger.
Next, coax her out of spontaneities,
Dangle conveniences, blinker her with a room.
Third, bluff her by showing who's lord of space and stars;
Pry from her every truth she knows about flying.
Fourth, to discredit everything that's growing,
Gloat over autumn, rub in the defeat of leaves.
Fifth, a contest of prayers, a collision of songs.
Finally, stage a show to spoof her gods
(But don't let her play them herself; a trickster has tricks).

WE [*exaggeratedly counting on fingers to mimic mannerism of aunts*]:
Point seven: if it is so grand a crisis,
Why itemize it like a laundry list?
Your plan of war is frivolous details.

THEY: We are the pedants of apocalypse.
A flood wells up through small specific sands.
So does this war: the age against the ages.
In case the six small sly maneuvers fail you,
We watchers will step in with sterner cures.
[*Aunts leave.*]

WE: O no, if all six fail, we'll let *her* let us
Let ourself loose in some Arcadian binge,
Escaping from maneuvers and from aunts.
End with a trial (where all sides yell their case,
She, they, and we, in beautiful confusion)
Before we judges make our own free choice.

Scene 2, FIRST TWO MANEUVERS*

THEY: What's "dryad" but a show-off word for splinter,
A girl-wisp shrugged into life from some boredom of wood?
The pride of such is splinter of a splinter;
Tell how you snapt it with Maneuver One.

WE: We had hoped she'd look so strange, so warped by tree-
      years,
Tourists would pay to stare at her from far.

THEY: Sweetened by fee, what's pride for but to swallow?

WE: They found
                she looks like anybody else.
Only that inner tune of hers is different.
But unseen innards sell no freak-show tickets.

THEY: So timber's waif proved non-negotiable?

WE: We tried a harder sell: not stare from far
But tease from near; let teen-age he-men frisk her
And sneak a feel or play good-natured contests
Like run-her-down with hot-rods.

THEY [*radiant with approval; moralizing voice*]:
                          Self-expression!
And tests of skill in peer-group competition.

WE: For laughs, they fed her manure, saying, "Make like a
      tree."

  * Crude hand-painted poster on rising curtain: "1st 2 MANEUVERS."
26

THEY: Sound group-dynamics. What went wrong?

WE: Kids loved it.
But the Better Business Bureau closed us down
As phoneys—when they found no dryad, only
Air and a clientele that aired their stench out.
Yet she's to us as real as
                                    you, for instance.

1st AUNT [*to other two*]:
Divert them from that sector. Get out quick
Before they stumble on what's really up.

[*Aunts leave left-stage. Dryad enters right-stage, trailing flowers
and singing to concealed music.*]

SHE: The reaching out of warmth is never done.
To see around the bend, to see around,
Through ice to see a poppy wink you on,
Entangle with the tentacles of light
And nudge a green unkemptness up from night,—
The mixed-up splice of things, the all, the one.
          Mix in, mix in, and weave a blurring Other.
          Give all—keep twining in—and you may get
          A more-than-all: three dance a strict quartet,
          And pairs are threes (O Eros, unseen brother),
          And even grapes, so single in their glowing,
          Mix with a twin from sky (O wine-god, flowing);
          The reaching out of warmth is never done.
What reaching up, though old, can still astound?
Persephone is stirring underground.
Stretching up drowsily through melting snow
See how each calyx opens, row on row
(Whole hillsides now, soon half a planet sighing);
Each flower-throat "O" exhales her wakening yawn.

What twining in with death is never dying?
Till flame is burnt and water drowned,
The reaching out of warmth is never done,—
The mixed-up blur of gods, the good black sun.

WE: "The gods"—that's all we hear. For once define them.

SHE: Dolphin and resin glitters of delight.
A god is simply what is unconditioned,
Wonder to faith and question-mark to science,
A nuisance imp to plan-worlds—call it "freedom,"
Or "superstition." Synonyms today.

WE: These needed nuisances, are they forever or changing?

SHE: An overflowing pause
As hills are waves.
A static undulance
As waves are hills.
                    Have seen mere change:
                    The color seeped away.
                    Have seen mere stance:
                    The pampered sentry slumped.
Through wave through hill
Through changing changelessness,
Our fated
Spontaneities.

WE: Who ever heard of strict
Quicksilver?
What'll we do with the stuff?

SHE [*ambling across and pressing our hands*]:
Hold tight what spontaneities are left you,
And barricade them from improved technology.
Manipulated needs, kind as a mother
Robot, push around the button-pushers.

WE: The tough line failed; here comes Maneuver Two.
To ease you from the coiled up core of things,
We offer you distraction's mezzanine
And of synthetics all the plush and chock-full.

SHE: Because you are anonymous, you poach from
Possessiveness your pale identities,
The pastel shades of being. Yet rouged as "vital";—
Corpses and apples sport as bright a cheek.

WE: We give; you change. Come, tree girl, leave your blur
    world.
Wall out those vista-curves of sprout and flux.
Come try edged contours, try our blinkered vistas,
Try all these feelings of solidity
We paste together when we say, "A room."
       A cube of wall-to-wall swaddling. A square
        Wedding-ring to sanction the hug of swag.
O how enough to praise a room's bonanzas,
So pat, so tailored! And so muffled from
The probes—the ice-winds—from between the suns.

SHE: Slim-streaking as the afterglow of trout,
The same warm winds cascade through suns through veins.
I do not ask the earth-beats at my feet
If strummers or if echoes of my pulse.

WE: There's strumming before echo. Which is us?

SHE: No matter if immortals are your echoes
Or you are theirs. Each is the other's shadow.

WE: Is that what you call spontaneities?
We do not need shadows of shadows;
We do not need such gods to link us;
Enough that the foursquareness of a room
Assures us there's no cave of loneliness
Parties and central heating cannot fill.

SHE: Fuller and lonelier than walls account for,
Your rooms are asteroids turned inside out.
Their glows,
　　　　　　aimed inward as a blindman stares,
Touch only through the icy Braille of doors.

WE: There is ice no herds, no house-warmings can reach.

SHE: Tune-links, secret tune-links all around you,
The same if strummers or if echoers,
Are reaching out—unwall your heart—to warm you.
To warm but not—wall up your heart—to herd.

WE: Unwall or wall?

SHE:　　　　　　　The mixed-up warmth of freedom
Links without chaining.

WE:　　　　　　　Other freedom-talkers
Vend a solution or salvation. You
Don't solve or save but—what?

SHE:　　　　　　　　The one evasive tune.
[*starts her ballet*]
Don't trudge apart the unsolved dance of things.

[BALLET INTERLUDE: *dryad is duplicated by big distorting wall-mirrors, as if she were several different dancers. Each time she dances tauntingly between us, we vainly grab not her but her mirror images. At end of ballet, exit dryad dancing, followed by the pursuing "we."*]

Scene 3, BIG DOINGS *

[*Two painted backdrops descend. Left painting: a machine, launching aircraft to orbit around golden star. Right painting: a human hand, sending paper airplane in playful circle around yellow butterfly. We and they, whenever speaking, stand under left painting; she under right painting. We enter on left, wearing space suits; aunts follow.*]

WE: Objective tools, free of everything personal,
Conduct experiments that cannot lie.
[*brandishing cameras and telescopes*]
With these we'll map the furthest galaxy.
Maneuver Three will show her who rules space.
[*We hold onto painted aircraft; wire pulls it and us to ceiling.*]

THEY [*pointing up proudly*]:
Big doings! Engines
Still higher. Up there
Stars (golden and flying)
Challenge. Again, again
Up reaches will, male, steel.

[*pointing contemptuously down at paper plane on right painting:*]
          Paper-flimsy below
          Is grove-child's aimless aim:
          Trifle of squandered graces,
          Confetti of false starts,
          Ashcan of reveries.

* Large bulletin board announces "MANEUVER 3, BIG DOINGS IN SPACE."

[*Dryad enters and stands at right painting. She speaks the three Aldébaran stanzas (her three speeches that follow) with slow stately gentleness, accompanied by music off-stage, and folds paper into shape of toy hat and later of toy plane.*]

SHE: One day men will get up before the sunrise,
Night-air still eerie with Aldébaran,
And gravely wear the pointed cardboard hats
(Spangled with cookie-shapes from astro-textbooks)
That dwarfs and jugglers caper in at fairs
To make the yokels gape at lore of stars.
And each hat pointing toward Aldébaran.
I say there are strong winds between the atoms,
Strong lonelinesses all around each textbook,
And these, that day, will blow your hats toward ashcans,
Will waft or dip them as the atoms frisk,
Pleading, "Aim nearer, nearer, tenderer;
Find more in less, the highest in the inmost."

THEY: Mere voice of trance and play.
[*falling on knees before engine of left painting*]
            O Bentham, builder of cities,
            Has Eros bridged space, has
            Play honed precision tools?
            Unlaunchable was trance. Then
            Launch engines. Doings!

SHE: You'll rally back, O fatuous Man Invictus;
How masterful you'll snag the winds of space
Right through their manes and braid them into networks
And engineer far lonesomeness away
And knead cowed space into your cookie-dough.
Then how they'll soar, the pointing hats will soar,
Your hero-hats will stab Aldébaran.
Then burn your corpses or the pigs will eat them,

Because the graves that day shrug tombstones off
And gape astounded at Aldébaran.

THEY [*derisive voice*]: But you?

SHE: But I (because the much is in the little
And cosmos hangs upon a feather's fate)
Will twist my hat into a paper airplane
And aim it nearer than Aldébaran
And skim it round a yellow butterfly.

.   .   .

THEY: Do you think that kind of fooling around
Will fly you further than they?

SHE [*gravely*]: Not further. Higher.

[*Wire lowers us back from ceiling. We get out of space suits,
throw maps on floor in disgust.*]

WE: The higher we traveled, the more we stayed on the
      ground.
[*confusedly*]
We still don't get it.

THEY: What did each of you
Find on the maps your perfect tools brought back?

WE: Each only the lines of his own guilty face.

THEY: [*leaping up with hypodermic needles*]
Her lies have done it again. But this time
                              [*stabbing her*]
                              truth serum.
Make her confess all she knows of flying and magic.

[*Aunts leave. Rest of scene is our interrogation of her under third-degree spotlight. We confidently brandish hypodermic needle of serum.*]

WE [*to each other*]:
Infallible needle, perfect as those tools were.
We fabricate only the best hardware
For handling hearts. From now on, all she tells us
Can't help but be the truth. So ask her everything.
        [*to her*]
        Why is our up so down? Our speed so treadmill?
[*We hand her writing-paper and turn interrogation-light brighter.*]

SHE: I'll tell such truth you'll wish I left you lies.
[*She tears up paper and stares straight into spotlight, which, as if by coincidence, dims.*]
Truth is not graph and glare but fluff and side-glance.

WE: We want, as first truth, up-beat of your dance,
To harness it, so it can make us fly.

SHE: Flight has as many meanings as one brings it.

WE: Elusive is, how webbed your waywardness,
How secret-linked your random fluffs and whims.
That web, that rhythm!—sieves of chemic jargon
Can't sift that upwardness from sap. As if
Our jetted gallivantings winged that longing's
Mere quantity and bogged its quality.

SHE: Lambaste with niblicks, till your femurs falter,
The know-how marshes. Useless. Gimmicks wangle
Everything up except that wistfulness.

WE: Derricks lift best. What other kind of lifting?

SHE: Planes are but swifter kind of trudge, not flight.
True flight is trance, airy and earthy both,
A feathering of arterial skyward lurch,
When body embodies more than body, yet
Seamlessly one. The key, the holy rape,
Is the word "yet,"
                              outside clay "yet" right here.

WE: That splits our wish, confused at touch of skin.
You told us truth of flight; small good it did us;
Confess a further truth: why can't we touch?

SHE: A prying epoch but no touch direct.
Because you learn by searchlight, not by feel,
Even your seers flash thin, like comet's rumpus,
Or mull on kickshaws as a camel chews.
Asthmas of book-dust between sight and insight;
A glove for clasps; for ripeness, cellophane.
I have lived trees more tactile one short day
            (The bobbed-on twigs of daybreak, sag of noon,
            Till lane on lane of muted evening sweetness)
Than all your lifelong mobile fingertips.
Touch? Bees won't touch your brilliantest glass flowers.

WE: Beneath our jaunty modern air we ache with
An old hereditary desert-plague,
Called conscience-versus-touch, abstraction-versus-meat.
Our clasps are sties; not God, not meat; God's dung.
The more the aunts lock out, the more the pillows
Let in,—our contradictions, vengeance-browed.
            Still one more truth: how scrap these chains that
                                                    ground us?

SHE: When will the galley-slaves of birth-guilt hammer
Their chains to rungs, their nerves to stairs of fire?
Out of blood's Pliocene and shark-reefed surf,

Upright lurch from oarlocks, up bleak beach
Where every final self-confronting duels.
There now let guilt's long wave pound out, subside.

WE: There radiantly end all tears, all limits?

SHE: Even then, slick off the tears of tragic limits
Never. From rain, from curse, from sullen roots
Radiance darkly earns the bloom you bless.

WE [*visibly struggling to recover our complacency*]:
We'll solve that mishmash on dissecting tables.

SHE: Dissect away. Then patch with soul-molasses.
I see twin midgets at a circus grandstand
Pummel each other with bladders of science and faith
While, way up there, the wine-god, belching
An ode to tragic joy, spills popcorn down on both.

WE: Both blend. The tractor and the galaxy.

[*Two new backdrop paintings descend: gear-studded tractor and modern drive-in church; latter is haloed by an encircling galaxy with bright light-bulbs as stars. We touch tractor at first line that follows, church at second.*]

Two clockwork systems. Gears emit new goodies,
While—for our Sunday breadline, Sunday blood bank—
The stained-glass freezer stores dead flesh-and-blood.
          Science or faith: two saviors proffered you.
          What third choice could you want beyond these two?

[*In each of her two quatrains that follow, she likewise touches tractor at first line, church at second.*]

SHE: One savior is Hygeia's germproof lap,
And one Maria's galaxy of hope.

My star is earth, unsaved and doomed:
Disheveled gods from mortal bloom-dust bloomed.
>Godless joy is test-tube sap;
>Joyless God is desert drouth.
>My true, my joyful wine-god grape
>Is south.

WE: Sky or mortality?
Old polarity.
Tree-girl, what gesture heals the old dispute?

SHE: Lechery of growingness.
>Toward airiness, toward earthiness.
>Gesture of twig and root.

WE: That disreputable wine-god of yours,
What does he answer when harangued on virtue
Or else its new name, Scientific Method?

SHE: Old Bakkhos bellows:
[*Bakkhos lines spoken by deep male voice off-stage*]
>>"Virtue? Or detachment?
There's more morality and truth in coupling
Rabidly on crossroads with a hyena with crab-lice
Than to chew cud with a highminded ox
Or squawk objectivity with a capon."

WE: Our heroes!—who dares call them
>>less than beasts?

SHE: As fellow heroes, fowl and bovine called on
Akhilles; he "cased" both of them and snorted:
>[*male voice of Akhilles off-stage:*]
>"Better the poor slave of a poor master
>Than king of a drive-in church or a filing system."

WE: What's going on here? Are you ratting on
Religion and science?

SHE: What *you* call science. What you *call* re-
                       ligion.

[*She crosses stage to tree, leans on it carelessly, and strums lyre
hanging from it to sing next three lines:*]

SHE: Between the tractor and the galaxy,
I comb my hair and lounge against my tree
And watch a yellow butterfly slip through.

WE [*pointing at both backdrop paintings*]:
Two cold contraptions, closing in on you.
They'll meet, there'll be an end to wings and jigs.

SHE: No need my calling,
                       yet,
                              to Aphrodite.
No need at all for gods so mighty.
Not only love—mere wisp of fun suffices
To dodge your frown.
I tell you, no computer organizes
The pranks and chipmunks of the bounce of twigs.

WE: They won't much care for pranks in Middletown.

[*Saying this, we switch off interrogation-light with resigned gesture and give up. Disgustedly we leave stage. She remains alone.
Interval of unseen wild exultant music, preparing ahead for the
short-line wine-god dithyrambs that end scene 3.*]

SHE: From now on, courage is my only tree,
Aërial trunk, as hard to hack as granite.

Tree-shelled, I dared no brawl for truth or song;
An ax forced both on me; pain made me strong.
Pain carves defeated clay to joyful shapes.
          Gods who preside at wine's nativity,
          Old sorrows of the wine-press agony,
          Sustain in me, when autumn strips the planet,
          The self-surpass of the defeat of grapes.
Courage I learnt the day I overheard
The senile outcast wine-god (doddering by
With somehow springy step) drool in his beard
(Amid deriders) this rejoicing cry:

                    [*male voice of Bakkhos off-stage:*]

               "An old man with flowers
               Is lament without sorrow.
               Delighted dust
               Perpetrates noon.
               Sound of reaping
               Even in springtime
               Sings inside me
               Without sorrow.
               Soft wind,
               I am not afraid to end."

WE [*heavily stomping back in*]:
Noon is a scandal
Of hiccups and flowers.
Disgrace without sorrow
Is a wind of pariahs
And weaves clamminess in.

SHE [*pushing away our above words*]:
Those words then too; but he without hearing:

[*male voice off-stage:*]

"Once I was afraid.
My feet felt toads.
Now all is a wreath:
I weave everything in.
An exile at noon
Is a flowering sorrow.
An old man with flowers
Is warm to the end."

Scene 4, SONGS AS ACTIONS:

THE AUTUMN MANEUVER*

[*We and she in yard outside garage; we separated from her by side-curtain, around which we eavesdrop; she facing tree with dark late-summer foliage.*]

SHE: Outside my window is a wall of green;
I see no higher than a tree is tall;
I see no further than a leaf allows;
Where is October and the harvest-glean?
I hear no thud of plum beyond the wall;
Between the grape and me, a wall of green;
How long since last I was a god and rose
As cadence of the wine-press festival?
      [*twining with tree*]
      I knew, from inside once, this very green;
      It was my skin; and tingling I recall
      How just this tint, when just so rich it flows,
      Would drain my roots to feed my tallest boughs.
      Seeing now such fullness, my whole body knows
      So deep in summer is not far from fall.

[**Enter aunts.**]

THEY [*to us*]:
Three lost maneuvers: humbling, bribing, flying.
Autumn—the fourth—will make her own hopes fail.
We planted her old tree-home, before fall,
Outside her window so she'll watch it failing.

  * Highway billboard: "MANEUVER 4, THE DEFEAT OF LEAVES."

Make her howl dirges on the death befalling
What grows. Triumphant metals feel no fall.

[*Aunts rip off side-curtain that separated her from us, redrape it
so as to hide tree from audience, and leave stage. At our fourth
line below, we restore tree to view; tree has meanwhile been
changed from late-summer to autumn, with a single large red
leaf. During first two lines, we point at painted backdrop of
modern apartments.*]

WE [*to her*]:
In the conditioned kits we rarely leave,
Our in-grown Spring need brave no season's falling.
Yet out we've stept to see your old tree failing,
And so to strip you of your old belief,—
While clinics tape-record, without your leave,
Melodies maundered for your own relief:
        Three voices of autumn (from your tree-harp falling
        As crisscross as the drift of falling leaf).

SHE: The first two are the autumn dialogue
Of Ouranos and Gaia, sky and earth,
The father and the mother you forgot.
First, Father Ouranos, as if serenading:—

[*First and second autumn songs—staged as dialogue—are ema-
nating from tableau vivant of sky serenading and then embrac-
ing earth; sky as male actor, reaching down from suspended cot-
ton cloud; earth as actress in wheat-costume, reaching up from
autumnal orchard.*]

        If through a wind I ripple every tide
        With such a wave as rattles every quay,
        It is to haunt the true lost flesh they hide;
        All seas, all soils but sheathe my bride from me.

Her skirt of colored seasons crowns her thighs
And circles round the lunar tune she sways.
—O loose your sweet green locks with drowsy grace
And slowly brush their warmth across my eyes.

Twisting your shoulder-blades beneath the plow
That fondles you when apple twigs are bent,
Deep in your hills you would not huddle so
If you believed how sad I am you went.

Then let no princeling of the apricots
Excite you with the ripeness of the year.
His nectared cheeks must burst; your courtier rots;
My snows are on his trail, will soon be here.

And yet am sun. I nibble listlessly
A ghat of all the wives of all my whims.
Autumnal tawny harems burn for me.
Such games will not distract me from your limbs.

Call to me dawdlingly when summer falters.
Attract me bitterly through molten grain.
I am your sky; look up; my clouds are altars
To worship you with desecrating rain.

SHE: Now earth's reply, invoking the autumn instant:—

Then touch the park; the leaves are stained to lure you.
The leaves are spread on winds they fan befòre you.
They drained the summer, and their veins prefèr you,
Dark with the season they are droning for.

Then bring the heavy dying they prefer.
Each painful fruit is hanging heavier.
Why pause when loveliness grows lonelier

And love is just as melting as it looks?
There's but one touch that all the ripeness lacks:
You are the instant; you are waited for.

Then never wait when flutes of foliage bear you
Home on the homeward tune they always bore.
Fear not at all the twigs of flame they bear.
These never meant to be a barrier.
The lovely are as lonely as their gleam,
The lonely just as loving as they seem,
The fruits as melting as they always were:
There is a fondling they are furtive for.

Then touch my park. The leaves have spread befòre you
The green they drained, the darkness they prefer.
Come to the leaves, reach out and touch them all.
Bring to the smoldering year, that hovers fòr you,
The hovering instant love is dawdling for:

There's not one leaf that does not long to fall.

· · ·

WE: Your swarthy Gaia, all these Levantines,
Keep sidling up to hawk Olympic tours
While we watch our purse.
                                    You owe us one more autumn.
But bring myth up-to-date first. For example,
Just what was Aphrodite up to after
The clock struck One A.D.? Fill in such blanks.
Come edify us with some wholesome ballad.

SHE: A short-line ballad makes me scan my sister
By her more parvenu short Roman name.
Venus Venus Sister Venus.

WE: Sister? Then Ouranos strews seed like autumn!
As heard on TV's "Myth Made Easy" hour,
His famous wound strewed blood as much as foam.
We know whom foam bred on the sea. But blood?

SHE: Blood bred the tree nymphs on the land. Love's sisters.
(And bred the Furies, fortunately gone.)
My father dies in every leaf that bleeds,
And every leaf will find my mother's lap.

WE: Sing Venus, but make her inspirational:
Prize-pupil's recitation-piece in pigtails
Of fallen female salvaged by repentance.

[*Meanwhile dryad slips on costume of a modern "Magdalen"; perhaps flaunted furs, long and tight black evening dress. Swinging
long cigarette holder, she strides up and down in rhythm with
her "BALLAD OF MAGGIE JONES":*—]

SHE: Is it HER voice, repenting repentance,
                 We hear when a mattress groans?
                 What goddess haunts the downstairs couch
                 Whenever Smith dates Jones?

                 Let other birds chirp for your prizes
                 On wrists that have never known grief.
                 I sing for the sons who'll defy you
                 And the daughters of Venus, not Eve.

                 Lost children, reach out for each other;
                 Respectable joys fade to junk
                 When a girl is a jigsaw-puzzle
                 And a boy is the solving chunk.

                 Cold nights and callous mornings;
                 Dirt clings to all we own.

          Then cling to each other, soiled children;
          Cry we must, but at least not alone.

WE: Not what we ordered. Fool. Misunderstood.
Croon how love's goddess, renamed Magdalena,
Now wears low heels and brings sick soldiers water.

SHE: What's Venus up to anyhow
                Now that her doves are crows?
                She plays THE BALLAD OF MAGGIE
                                        JONES.
                And here is how it goes. . . .

                After I give them lust or birth,
                They all crawl out and cry.
                I tuck them back, they still won't stay
                In any womb but sky.

                My love needs dollars, his needs souls,
                Mine is the cheaper fee.
                My quicksand hugs for half a night,
                His for eternity.

                I've nothing at all to heal the sick
                Except myself to share,
                My few warm inches of cosiness
                Against his eons of air.

                So what could I do but join his troupe?
                My others took and paid.
                My others took and went. He gave,
                Seduced my soul, and stayed.

                What else could I do but bathe his feet?
                His magic seemed stronger than mine—
                Till Smith's boy, Judas, rang my bell,
                More drunk with the bread than the wine.

Young Judas kissed my breasts and said,
"Eternity's too old.
I hate the skies I cannot touch.
I hate his love; it's cold."

WE: Too long for a ballad. Only three more stanzas allowed.

SHE: That Judas wisdom freed me.
        Glum centuries ensued:
        The lioness thrown to the Christians,
        Venus crucified.

        Then why do I bring them water
        And nurse each time their ache?
        Because my only creed is
        Warmth for its own crude sake.

        I don't much like humanity.
        My love is lilt, not vow.
        I warm, each time, not mankind but
        One near one here and now.

[*Speaking above last stanza at exit-door, she leaves stage with air of leaving for a rendezvous.*]

WE: That was all a distraction to make us forget her promise
Of three autumn voices; we've counted only two, and
She's playing for time because the third voice, being
Dirge of the seasons, is the forlornest.
The seasons: door-guards of Olympos once,
Demoted now to functionless adornments
In the conditioned Spring we rarely leave,—
Their shattered circle
[*shrugging at re-entering dryad*]
            hers.

SHE [*back in Greek tunic*]:
Voice of the seasons, the obsessed returners,
Voice of the seasons (to leaves, in leaf-drift rhythms):—*

> Like actors in a death-scene played with poise
> Lest rant make critics smile or scare small boys,
> You fall. No blood, no blenching.
> Only the dry red wrenching.

> Leaves on panes,
> Wistful for the green so briefly borrowed.
> Then the rain's
> Fiddling on the twigs so newly sorrowed.

> Leaves on loam,
> Dead children knocking to be let back in.
> Each has been
> Tree-top-dizzy while so high from home.

> Sweet and swift,
> Your first careen on air; then crushed to be
> Waif of drift
> Between the tractor and the galaxy.

> Yet joy is what they crush you to,
> The work machine and the world machine.
> Kiss of the wine-press festival, renew
> Red lips of autumn with the pledge of green.

---

* Her third autumn voice gets acted as alternation of long and short cadences, moodily drifting, addressed to red leaf on tree between back-drops of tractor and church-centered galaxy. Actor intonation and off-stage music are low and slow when accompanying short, heavy-voweled lines like "Leaves on loam"; high and spry when accompanying long, quick-voweled lines like "Dead children knocking to be let back in."

They'll have their autumn too,
Machine and machine.
Next year not they re-green,
Outfading you.

Flawless their clockwork-flash;
Leaf drags with loam;
Falling from speed to ash,
Not they fall home.

Leaves in space:
Vintage whose radiance outshines a ray's.
Leaf on steel:
Rainbow whose year outspins a wheel.

Spin death and beauty (year now sere, now heady),
Opposites—feuding, fornicating—in
Green already
Reddening.

Not godless joy or joyless God,
Machined as "good for" or as "good,"
But doom made sweet in art and
Bloom out of bloom-dust gardened.

Fuse death and beauty (leaf now red, now green),
Infinites in a wisp of sheen;
Fuse forth the specter no mirrors mirror,
That last of the temples, that innermost terror,

Between the tractor and the galaxy
That marble hammered from mortality:
The clay which is the self-surpass of clod,
The gods who are dishevelment of God.

Then warmth is what the clockworks crush you to,
The wheels and rays;

O fullness of the festive wine-press, strew
A throb of colors through the ice of space.

Then flutter the green joy of your red going;
A color was a thirst when you were growing;
A color is a promise today when you fall.
Triumphant falling leaf, you are the strongest thing of
all.

ACT II

(INTERMISSION BEFORE AND AFTER ACT II)

Scene 5, SONGS AS ACTIONS:

THE COLLISION CONTEST *

[*Curtain remains down, we in front of it during our opening speech to each other.*]

WE: Gloatings on death and autumn but renew her.
We rubbed her face in; she sang twice as strong.
Let the grand plan unwind the Fifth Maneuver,
A duel fought with her own weapon: song.
By our own sweepstakes we are swept along
And cannot stop the wheel, whose turnings prove her
Each time a more unfathomable mover.
      Now we, she, they—as gong collides with gong—
      Sing out our prayers in contrapuntal throng.

[*Curtain rises. Stage in three partitions, aunts in one, dryad in another, we in third. All kneel for our respective creed-songs; aunts beside human-size bird cage; dryad beside tree of previous scene, now with Greek lyre hanging where last leaf had been; we beside tractor-galaxy paintings of scene 3. Contest opens with "THE AUNT CREED":*]

1st AUNT:
Decode by force the mixed-up hint of things,
Extort this truth which every scalpel brings:

ALL 3 AUNTS:
Cages teach useful lessons to daft wings.

---

* Scoreboard, headed "MANEUVER NUMBER," with blank for interchangeable numbers; after pause of whirring noises, "5" clicks into place.

53

2nd AUNT:
At times we ogle a trapeze that swings
With plagues of foolish, feathered carolings;
We rescue it with rocks that soundness flings;

ALL 3:
Cages teach useful lessons to daft wings.

3d AUNT:
Catch childhood young with rings
Round its imaginings;
Dry up those springs.
Pull it with dazzling strings;
Pelt it with Fact that pings
Whatever sings.
Because rash necks invite the fist that wrings,

ALL 3:
Cages teach useful lessons to daft wings.

1st AUNT:
And yet,
        though brows are stuffed with parrotings,
Some traitor-pulse unkings
(In brows beyond our stings,
In songs beyond our slings)
Wisdom with wonderings,
Soundness with flutterings;—

ALL 3:
In vain, in vain do cages preach to wings.

[*Spotlight shifts to dryad, speaking* "THE TREE PRAYER":]

SHE: You high ones, old ones, watching two by two
Wherever shrineless gods are exiled to,

Send down your lightning. But your olive too.
Cool whisper of the ages, not the age,
Expand the shallows of men's anchorage,
Apprentice them to more than they can hear.
You earth-deep resonance they dare not hear,
Be everywhere, like fragrance of the orange,
Yet single and sonorous as its root,
Till lives are sweet and inward as an orange,
And every death a quilt of leaves on root.

[*Spotlight shifts to us; aunts temporarily enter our partition.*]

1st AUNT [*to us, with melting voice*]:
Now your turn; crow a credo we'll be proud of.
[*to 2nd aunt, with crisp military voice:*]
You check for deviators,
[*to 3d aunt:*]   you for doubters.

WE: We want life horizontal; what
Is vertical we roll down flat.
Our strength is as the strength of ten
Because we are replaceable men.
Replaced from infinite supplies,
What's duplicated never dies.
Jam-packed and yet frictionless
On the oil of civic bliss,
Perpetual motion standing pat,
We look like humans but we're not.
We are ball-bearings in disguise.

[*Looking satisfied by our recited credo, aunts return to their own partition.*]

WE [*furtive voice, to each other*]:
It never happened again, it was like this;
Just once, at snooze of aunts, when sap kicked out,
We were backsliders. That hour, pride in size

(Near dinky vines)
Seemed but a piling up of what won't grow.
Drunk in the grapeless reel and strut of splurge,
We sagged like puffballs belched by their own bulge.
(Now near her vines
Our fit returns.)
Now when, guffawing in cahoots with wheels,
We boil whole countrysides in eight-lane tar,
What goat-foot smears lewd shapes on it at night?
Our smooch with mammon sulks in paradise
Because of some bleached moon we hanker after,
Some glassblower's lost algebra of shimmer.

[*Aunts re-enter grim-faced; we snap to attention, eager-voiced again.*]

WE: But quick rebounding, bland and pink as ever,
From that last wobble of that backslide hour,
Let's all intone the modern litany,
The positive-edited digest of Great Books.

[*Now comes "THE MODERN LITANY"; tone of incantation; instead of enjambement, we-spokesman pauses solemnly after every verse-line, regardless of punctuation:—*]

Aunts, guardians, toilet-trainers, lend us your deafness
To prejudice and make us nonconformists
Like everybody else. Tell Sparta
These truths we hold to be semantic blurs.
For we are alone among mankind
In combining free individualism (that is, personalized station-
                                                    ery)
With sense of community (our folk-dance classes).
Lead us not into deviation, but
Make us feel guilty near No Trespass signs
As we make guilt-ridden those who trespass against us.
Give us this day our daily treadmill

Of keeping up with those who keep more up,
But deliver us from psychosomatic heart-attack
By granting free parking to customers. For thine is
The working-hypothesis that moves the sun and the other stars.

. . .

SHE: The air clogs thick with creeds; that was
[*pointing to where our litany came from*]
the third one.
All rise like incense: crookedly—

WE [*looking upward*]:   —and twining
Their incompatibles (ours hers, theirs hers, theirs ours)
Into collision songs. Each song two voices.

THEY: Each song not pause nor dream but song-as-action;
We all as rhythms and those rhythms wars.

[*The separating stage-partitions drop and thereby re-unite actors
for song-duels that follow, each duel with new backdrop. Now
comes first collision song, entitled "LINE AGAINST CIRCLE";
backdrop of big barred windows opening onto vista of stars and
clouds.*]

WE SPOKESMAN:
Solidity rushes on.
We move in a moving maze.
Vertigo—praise it—alone
Stays. Cling to it tight.
Man is a flare-up of clay;
Shall he wait to be snuffed, shall he run?
"Run!" the windows invite;
Express, expand while we may.
Man is a skidding of light
Bogging in clouds, a daze
Of longings and fruit, a stone

Thrown by thrower unknown.
Praise elation of flight.

SHE: Solidity rushes on—
              Brittle ghost at play—
              Onto the window bars.
              "Stand, wait!" they invite;
              Compress to the core while you may.
              Center and farthest sun,
              Thrower and throw are one;
              Pattern stays.
              Alternate heart-beat of light
              Grooms and dishevels stars.
              Rest in that heart. Praise
              Repose of flight.

[*Now second collision song, called "GOLDEN BANALITY, PRO
AND CON"; dryad and single we-spokesman alternately address
paper sun swinging overhead.*]

SHE: Who here's afraid to gawk at lilacs?
Who won't stand up and praise the moon.
Who doubts that skies still ache for skylarks
And waves are lace upon the dune?

WE: But flowering grave-dust, flowerlike snow-dust,
              But tinkling dew, but fun of hay,
              But soothing buzz and scent of sawdust
              Have all been seen, been said—we say.

SHE: BANALITY, our saint, our silly:
The sun's your adverb, named "Again";
You wake us with it willy-nilly
And westward wait to tuck us in.

WE: Trite flame, we try so hard to flout you,
                But even to shock you is cliché.
                O catastroph-i-cal-ly dowdy!
                O tedium of gold each day!

SHE: Who's new enough, most now, most youngest
Enough to eye you most again?
Who'll love the rose that love wore longest,
Yet say it fresher than quick rain?

WE [*to her*]:   You'll see. You'll say. You'll find the word.
                Even we must lilt then, willy-nilly,
                TRAPT by one banal triple-chord
                Of woman, sun, and waterlily.

   .   .   .

SHE: And here's the magnet
[*touches lyre*]   to compel that trap,
Eking out essences you lost in you.

WE: Being so compelled, our old lost self wakes up,
Lost childhood of the hour before the aunts.

THEY [*to each other*]:
Step in to save the singing-contest from her;
And stop their buried self from fountaining.

[*Now third collision song, called* "THE LOST SELF." *Two speakers, fussing with tea pots: young child (i.e., we-spokesman in child costume) and 1st aunt.*]

CHILD: Underground-rivers ripple.
            Ripples are sometimes heard.
AUNT: Child, don't hear them.
            Sit down, tea is served.

CHILD: People get used to each other.
               Sometimes this leads to harm.
AUNT: Elsewhere. Here's a
                              Potful; cover it warm.

CHILD: Younger, were years more under?
               Later, less haunted by blue?
AUNT: Patience; soon now
                              You will be deaf to them too.

CHILD: Once in a lifetime, buried
               Rivers fountain and call.
AUNT: Child, child, hear the
                              Daily kettle boil.

CHILD: Once; and who follows, touches
               Sand? Or gods? Or—tell!
AUNT: Child, stop trembling;
                              Porcelain cups may spill.

CHILD: Children whom tides have altered
               Live fierce and far. And drown?
AUNT: Quick, move nearer.
                              Tea is served, sit down.

[*We sit down at tea table with air of wallowing in total submission to aunts.*]

WE: Things being so, let them be with gusto so,
The lost self fevered off, the clambakes coming.

[*Now fourth collision song, "QUESTION AND ANSWER"; moon of green cheese swings from ceiling just out of our reach.*]

SHE: What do you see in the holy dread of the moonlight?
(Is it fire-lures dawdling on treacherous bogs?

Or a goat-leap you cannot quite glimpse through the fogs?
Or some slut of a goddess with red-eyed dogs
Hunting her lover, the moon?)
WE: Clambakes, clambakes on cranberry bogs;
            Cans piled up to the moon.

SHE: What do you hear in the holy dread of the moonlight?
(Some stalker whose reverent pouncing Yes
Affirms new unicorns of delicate loveliness?
When he kills, is it true that his beautiful claws caress
A painting, a poem, a moon?)
WE: Clambakes, clambakes on cranberry bogs;
            Hamburgers dimming the moon.

SHE: What do you feel in the holy dread of the moonlight?
(Are you drunk—till the hush of it chills your hair—
With the wager of man and his gay-tragic dare
To be moon of his own inner tide down here?
O pronounce me the wine of the moon!)
WE: It's clambakes, clambakes on cranberry bogs;
            Gumdrops all over the moon.

[*We leave stage, re-appear wearing—for this song only—gray flannel suits, placarded "MADISON AVENUE."*]

WE: We're not successful only but refeened.
As proved by our new song: "THE CULTURE-HUG BLUES."

[*This fifth collision song is begun by three "we" and resumed by aunts. Only one speaker at a time, but chorus at refrains. Nightclub backdrop. Actor intonation, and accompanying night-club orchestra, alternate between a vulgarly sentimentalized wail and an offensively raucous gloating, a marriage between oldfashioned pseudo-spirituals and modern advertising jingles.*]

WE:
We no longer starve culture; we SWITCH *
And hug it to death; the new PITCH
Is to croon antiquarian love-that-librarian CULture-hug blues.
When Status Quo feels safe enough to ITCH
For scripts that let it laugh at its own TWITCH,
What's big bold "beat" bohemia but Babbitt's latest NICHE?
When "liberal" is but a stance and "Tory" but a pout
And "radical" a tease to get still more for selling out,
When suburbs shriek with tongue-in-chic,
When ads for fads ape art-technique,
They all croon the CULture-hug blues.

If she isn't culture-snooty, there's a cooty on your cutie;
It's the duty of a beauty to be arty at a party,
Smarty with CULtural booze.
For Madison Avenue's guilt at its revenues,
What is the medicine? BLUES!
Not your mass-culture muse but our SENSitive muse,
Our anti-vulgarian, NEo-vulgarian, culture-hug blues.

If genius is an infinite capacity for faking PAINS,
Our Weltschmalz tears erase our huckster STAINS.
Art is an exorcism better than bell, book, and COUCH;
We're three blind Sensitive Plants, see how we wince, ouch
                                        ouch OUCH.
We've got to play with boors by day in order to stock the LAR-
                                        der;
We put to flight that guilt at night by hugging culture HARder;
A cultural ouch does more than the couch to purge that guilty
                                        ARdor.

* Each capitalizing of a whole syllable is stage directive for exaggerated
loudness and vowel-lingering; all non-capitalized syllables of such a line,
even those normally accented, get chanted in unaccented monotone.

From cash's clink aghast we shrink, to prove we can afFORD it;
With snoot held high we pass it by, because we've already
                                        STORED it;
High sen-ti-ment plus six per cent need never hug the SOR-
                                        did:—
Except in office HOURS, except in office HOURS.
Culture is like a FOReign rug; we hate its looks but need its hug
To prove we can afFORD it, to prove we can afFORD it.

We're crisp executives at dawn, *poètes maudits* at dusk,
But even a sensitive weed must feed its HUSK;
The culture we hug is a culture for dusk, an afterthought cul-
                                        ture, a rarefied musk
And not for office HOURS.
That's why, no matter how soulful we wince,
Our culture-hug muse and your mass-culture muse
Are identical sisters under their skins:
Both whore with who can afFORD it.

[*Music stops; aunts take over stage, addressing audience and us.*]

THEY: That's local culture. True folkways now are global.
Although Dyspepsi-Coca tiffs replaced
A famous Pepsi toast two sages drank
Inside a tech-tech-techniculture kitchen,*
What counts is their shared faith: in gadget-fidgets.
Forget all dreams outside that common faith;
Keep parroting, "Relax all global tension."
Knife out the gray stuff in the frontal lobe;
It spreads contagious dreams and won't relax.

* Dispatch of July 27, 1959: "Today two of the world's leading statesmen and rivals—a vice-president, a dictator—exchanged Pepsi-Cola toasts
in Moscow, at an American kitchen-exhibit dedicated to their common
aim of industrial progress."

Take lower cultures: Greek or Britons. They
Had tension: at Thermopylae, at Dunkirk.
Relax—here come "THE GLOBAL LOBAL BLUES."

[*Music resumes in night-club background for aunt-song that now
follows. At "plastic bag," aunts play catch with plastic earth-globe;
at "snip," with surgeon-scissors.*]

THEY: Now when dacha nouveau-riche and hot-cha profit itch
Merge brands,
When brain-wash sociology and sublim-ad psychology
Join hands,
When Pepsi-Cola toasts unite vulgarians of all LANDS
And "peace" means the homogenizing global churn of kitsch,
You'll be FORCED to croon the global lobal blues.
First they toasted, THEN they tiffed; yet—through summit
OR through rift—
Here's a truth will never shift while any bureaucrat com-
MANDS:
Human heads will get short shrift from RObot hands.
So strike up all Rotarian proletarian pan-barbarian BANDS.
Progress is a PLAStic bag;
Come stick in your head and what AILS you will gag,
Gasping the BLUE-in-the-face blues.
When our propaganda spasms turn your isms into wasms,
We'll bag the earth in a PLAStic globe and disconnect your
frontal lobe
With our gadget-pop Agitprop air-jet-hop think-no-more blues.

In the oldfashioned day, to make citizens stay reliable pals of
big BROther,
There were salt mine and whip, but now we just snip the gray
stuff that causes the BOther.
That snip is metaphorical, its blade a doctored word;
For the pen of the rhetorical is mightier than the sword;

And the blanker the grin, the blander within,
When a tranquillized planet must spin to the din
Of the world-lobotomy blues.
Let justice wobble sloppily in monolith monopoly;
Forget about Thermopylae; let Hungary bleed properly;
Cringe happily, vox populi, and dream it saves your skin—
      While your culture-hug muse, when she muses on NEWS,
      Keeps keening these meaningless Mother Goose blues:

      "Little boy Geiger, come blow your horn;
      There's beep in the meadow, there's borsht in the corn.
      Rockabye fallout, on top of the show;
      When the wind blows you, the tuna will glow;
      When the nerve BREAKS, Humpty Dumpty will fall;
      Down will come baby, CULture and all."

.   .   .

[*Now scene's concluding song,* "IN THE MONTH OF MARCH
THE SNAILS CLIMB TENDER TREES"; *rendered by dryad
casually, slowly, undramatically; alone on dimmed stage:—*]

In the month of March the snails climb tender trees
To be nearer the Pleiades.
Grass fingers nab heat.
The fish jump for the fun of it.
Later the roses are willing to fall.
The wasted thistle-fluff isn't sorry at all.
A vineyard, met while walking, is a shelter
Good to hold to in that helter-skelter.
For fun—or food? or hooks?—life likes to twitch;
After the ice, it will not matter which.
After the ice, the feathers—once all throat—
Are shushed; the paraplegic lakes can not reach out.
And so, from hooked exuberance to numbed retreat,

The gamuts have no meaning; or, what they have of it
Encysts in chunky particulars,—
The specific timothy-grass, the ungeneralized tears,
The vineyard met while walking, a life-buoy of Here,
Good to hold, in wave on wave of Anywhere.

Scene 6, THE VAUDEVILLE
OF THE GODS *

[*As curtain rises, we are busy hammering up a stage within the stage.*]

WE [*to each other*]:
Since Crisis Five was inconclusive,
The master plan proceeds to Contest Six.
     (Final maneuver.
       If even this one leaves us in the dark,
       We'll leap the hedge.)
"To kill her gods by spoofing, stage them," said
The aunts. We'll do it. But not quite the way
They told us to. We're smart. Instead of doing
The work ourselves, we'll make *her* play each part.

[*Dressed as circus barker, we-spokesman addresses actual theater audience as his guests at oldfashioned vaudeville:—*]

WE-SPOKESMAN:
Sit down, a party, everybody welcome.
You should have seen her, that time, ventriloquizing
In song the carcass of Maggie Aphrodite;
Tell all your friends we own a pet that mimics
All kinds of foreign noises and mislaid gods.

---

  * Light bulbs in style of theater marquee, flashing:
         "CONTEST NUMBER SIX,
         FINAL MANEUVER,
         THE VAUDEVILLE OF THE GODS"

[*louder, via circus megaphone, while rest of "we" applaud*]
Oldfashioned vaudeville! D.P. from treeland—
Unwillingly, but waifs must sing to sup—
Will now impersonate some ancient famous clowns:
Gaga Kassandra, the only mortal in the show;
Then lock-kneed Artemis and bovine Hera;
Melpomene, the—haha—tragic muse;
And bluestocking Athena; ending with
A second time at bat for Aphrodite,—
[*to dryad*]
But this time clown her more convincingly;
Trouble with gods, their packaging is fogey;
Our outfit dares what's new (if first it's vouched for
By polls, committees, fund raisers, and Univac).
Let's trot *them* out in brandnew cartons.

SHE: Whom?

WE-SPOKESMAN:
Why, the gods. You'll wear the props we fixed for each.
[*handing her each costume as named*]
Kassandra: wild-haired wig and crystal ball.
Artemis: tweedy sportswoman with shotgun;
Plus knickers, labeled "girdle of chastity."
Hera: a cow mask. Muse Melpomene:
A mask of droopy lips and moulted lyre.
Pallas Athena: an owlish spinster lecturer.
In a bikini, your sister Aphrodite:
Purple lips, chalk cheeks, on cardboard sea shell,
Her hair looped like a certain private posing
That Botticelli peddles in plain wrappers.
. . . Aunts, have we your permission? Label it
Group-playground psychodrama, and educators
Won't dare not back it.

THEY: What? *She* play Greek ghosts?
Mere graves, but easier to burst than padlock.
Don't fool with superstitions; they might be loaded;
Count no man happy till . . . Well, all right, try it.
Just keep it clean; we know that bunch from there;
You give those people bathtubs what you think
They do with 'em put coal in 'em well really!

WE [*to her*]:
Come climb—hop, hop—this platform, or we'll haul you.
Tonight we'll give the hot-foot to the heavens
And see if we can goad them to retort.

THEY: Hail man-the-improver,
For his is the world without end. In techniculture
A few statistics more, one plumb-line further,
Then all wild heavens hacked by will, male, steel.

[*Aunts go sit inconspicuously in corner, from now on interrupt
only in crises.*]

WE: The show is on. Start with Kassandra.

[*Dryad, having meanwhile briefly fled from stage, is kicked and
pummeled back on, now wearing Kassandra costume and doubled
up with pain.*]

WE: Well groaned! Fall into funny convulsions. But this time
Soothsay us no doom; gasp us some Social Gain,
Some forward dash to Broadminded from Morbid.

[*Recovering herself with visible effort, she now throws herself
into each impersonation for its particular appropriate retort to her
tormentors.*]

KASSANDRA COSTUME:
Pollyanna Trojan seer foretells
Utopia for sure, foundation funds
Endowing therapists, whole teams of them,
To cure man of his dawn (all grit removed):—
      Have Klytaimnestra contact clinic soonest
      To channel her aggressions socially;
      Have marriage counselor talk it over calmly
      With Paris man to man—"the kids come first";
      While Dionysos signs the A.A. pledge.

WE: Next, mime the queen of forest holiness,
Whose furry nooks and furtive privacies
We urbanized right open like a clam.

ARTEMIS COSTUME:
I heard a huntress hunting you to tell you:—
      The first revolt, the lap of earth betrayed,
      Was yours the day you jerked her metals out,
      Obstetric to the technic interval,
      Full-cycled soon, full-cycled soon.

WE: Croak us no doom against robuster brashness.
Whiz rises straight and won't put up with cycles.

ARTEMIS COSTUME:
      The last revolt, revolt against revolt,
      Is ours the day the misused ore absconds
      (From every juke box, laundromat, motel
      One melting, sabotaging, homesick flow)
      Back, back into mines virginal once more.

WE: Not enough laughs; a gyp; take Artemis away,
The only frigid skirt in all of Bulfinch.
Next Mrs. Big, the boss's wife. Have Hera
Tell what a thrill it is to contact gods.

HERA COW MASK:
Here comes a matron with big udders, grumbling:—
>   It's gods gods gods, the nuisance of it, dropping
>   In at all hours, housework never done,
>   And me their snack bar. Men at least wear out,
>   But you should see immortal deadbeats munching
>   Ambrosia through infinity and lounging
>   An indestructible haunch on my best cloud.

WE: And now the tragic muse. Disqualified
For lack of course-points in Creative Culture
With audio-visual aids. Good riddance if
Verse dries into a snore and an allusion;
Genius has higher chores: to comment upon comments.
Stale muse, what modern voice—name one—was left you?

MELPOMENE MASK:
>   There was one singer and one singer only.
>   Traffic not quite drowns out his pledge and mine:—
Come, we but dreamt it; already the blood-trailing wings are
Healing, and so is each single one of the hopes.
Much, much greatness is still ahead; and whoever
Loved as we loved, must heavenward go as we go.
Then guide us, you hours of soul, so youthfully   solemn;
Stay with us, all you forebodings and pleadings of sky;
You too, you protectors whose love is to hover with lovers.
Stay with us till we are separate no longer. Unite us
Up there wherever it is the serenest reside;
There with those hints from the Father, the orbs and the eagles;
There with the muses, the homestead of lovers and heroes;
There
>   or down here, on an island dissolving toward spring,
Where we rejoin whom we love in the gardens we loved in,
Where music rings true and April wears daffodils longer
And the cycle of spirit begins all over again.

WE: Ruthless amid the alien corniness,
We'll flunk that song in both our schools of litcrit:
Diction embarrassing
                    (too blunt a passion
For quarterly urbanity to explicate);
Message escapist
                    (too little social significance
For weekly doomsday to detect a Trend).
So try more gods. Try Zeus's highbrow brain-child.
Pallas, admonish us with all the trimmings,
Those fine distinctions proving all sides wrong.

PALLAS ATHENA OWL MASK:
Here comes an owl with spectacles to hoot:—
        The upshot is to craze two sides, not only
        Your shout-for-new but rootless shout-for-roots.
        Unbalance breeds unbalance; some who hate you
        Are sick with soil-cult, sinister with blood-cant,
        Silly (against your drabness) with romance.
        Same modernisms, twinned as bump and hollow:
        Your humane anti-life, their murderous life-cult.
        The dance to Dachau starts from Wotan operas.
        Never confuse the gods from nature's vineyard
        With those from soured art,
                            daimonic with demonic,
        Olympos with a riffraff of plumed snakes.

WE: There's one you haven't mentioned. God in the singular.

ATHENA MASK:
        God? No, but gods!—we live ones tombed as evil;
        Your dead one churched as virtuously pale;
        Your gallantest earthman—man's the rarity—
        Banalized into just another god.
        . . . Yet what's less Greek than pedant posing pagan?

To find us excavate yourself, not Greece.
In your own skull, nine egos deep, lies Troy.

WE: Throw her out!—a classic! We, the general reader,
Adore great art that hits us where we live;
Trouble with classics, they cannot hold their audience. No won-
                                                                    der
Athena was a headache to her father.
. . . And now the climax; Aphrodite now.

[*We-spokesman struts with megaphone while dryad is off-stage changing to Aphrodite costume.*]

WE-SPOKESMAN:
We've stuffed, to parody the lover goddess,
[*fingering the re-entering dryad*]
These falsies for the evening's final show.
        [*to dryad*]
        First her birth; theme all bad poets echo.
        We've heard the muse. She goofed. Now no more poems;
        [*voice ear-splitting loud:*]
        Bray us some gag in honest shirt-sleeve prose
        About that birth.

APHRODITE COSTUME [*voice mild and low*]:
Blue silence. Thickening. Then the long slow ripple.
The waves lobbed one shared language at the headlands.
Who'd guess a girl-child's relevance to harvests?
Yet the nudged beach quivered
A consternation of breast-pale dances.
And from the shoreline up the dunes, a rumor:
"With muffled fins a saboteur has landed.
But no, not fins; only a calcified Oh,
A nothing, a housed echo." Who'd guess pulse there?
The first boy who pocketed the first

Sea shell, knapsack of wounds,
Was smuggling inland the singing birthpangs,
Staining the dry hills with droned foam.
Calamitous sweetness,
What purer wisdoms once walked a loveless earth?
Does loam hoard reveries from feverless ages
Before that flabbergasting lilt was born?
No land-sound but was changed forever after,
Rubbing with a new reverberation
The sheens of bloom, the taffetas of wind,—
Riddling the rhythms of the works of man
With added resonance of
Undertow.

THEY [*to us in sudden alarm*]:
You final heir, whom aproned eons dandled:
Sea groaned, and all's in jeopardy again,—
All decent neatness muddled by that birth.
Remember the war.

WE: What war?

THEY: Like Henri Quatre,
Helen of Troy thought Paris was worth a mess.

WE: Wise aunts, be wise some other time. A show's on.
[*to her:*]
Tape Aphrodite for a quote or two
About her Underground movement against technics.

APHRODITE COSTUME:
Here comes a sigh from a guerilla hide-out:—
        Thoughts, flat enough to stack in a police file.
        Muse, powdered into jars of instant art.
        Dehydrate all creation for your freezers,
        And still you can't create its vital part.

Ah him who'd slip unprocessed to my bower,
I'd giftwrap my untranquillizered heart.

WE [*to each other, resentful sarcastic voice*]:
        Ah him who'd slip unprocessed to her bower,
        She'd giftwrap her untranquillizered heart!
[*to aunts:*]
Rebut her provocation. The show can wait.
We love to savor how you collar swervers;
Convince her with polemical palaver.

THEY: We process scowlers and we re-tread skidders
For turnpikes of our sameness. Grooves of rush,
Anxieties of lag.
                Then crash.
                        Then aunties:
To help you help yourself to be mature.
We call it T.L.C. The friendly hairshirt.

WE [*to dryad, sanctimonious voice*]:
That's "tender loving care." The psalms and soap
Of cultured education. Many of us
In lab, a few—good fellows too—in church still,
Hobnob together in these same good works.

APHRODITE COSTUME:
God-cant or atheist brother-cant, the same
Bland plumbers to adjust you, snip snip snip.
An ecstasy of world lobotomy.

THEY: We smear the margarine of buddy-unction
On all men's slums, to grease them into grinning.
Out of the zippered womb of automation,
We'll clank a new humanity to swagger
The slogan true: "untouched by human hands."

APHRODITE COSTUME:
No "human hands" to thumb defiance,
No "moving parts" to trip compliance;
Autonomy goes out-of-print.
       Though white and black togs in alliance
       Would gray the outrage of love's purple tint,
       Yet one recidivist last glint
       Kicks out at sanctity and science.
One ornery faun-kick topples whole
Airtight utopias of benign control;
Panicky lab clerks yammer at the switch,
"The frog leg, gentlemen, declines to twitch."

WE: Next time more action in your acting, or it's
Back to garage straw for home talent week.
But give us pratfalls and it's dimes we'll toss you
And later a surprise-bouquet we're hiding.
[*to each other, whispering:*]
A custard pie, to crown the prima donna.

THEY [*to us*]:
Late; soon we'll be in nightgowns and in bed.
Last warning; jokes get out of hand. Was said once,
Gods manifest themselves in many forms,
Bring many matters to surprising ends.
The tang of seas and seasons, longed for, drowned for—
Propulsions wondered-at and wondered-after—
Is of the older rhythm: lure and nightmare.
Seal leaky graves, dear boys, by mastering
This quick synopsis of three thousand years:—
       Infected oceans had a flower once
       That had a poison-perfume had whole nations
       Raving and minstreling and drowning past
       Language's wondered-after boggy limits.

WE: What's language got that we should goggle after?
Why link its beats to Aphrodite's wriggles?

THEY: She fouled a harmless, tideless billion gallons
With that lewd swaying she brought from moon to sea.
Next day, along came song. Song dared beyond
Language itself to set the tides to words.
Song seized love's panting as a metronome.

WE: In school, song's what we scan.

THEY: No, song scans you.
The up and down of lung and heart and clock,
Scansion of flesh in endless ebb and flow,
Are but the spilt iambics of a song.

WE [*sniggering*]:
Also lust's in and out?

THEY: If you but knew
Love's dodges. Lust is but the firstborn of them.
How simple if she had no other trapdoor
Except her dark one. Song's her second quicksand.
In song all siren-mists condense as one,
All gods, all evils, tumbling headlong out of
Imagination's impossible genie-bottle.
Song is what a sea shell poaches from the heavens:
Immortality crammed in one sweet mortal cry.
        But armed with exorcism, labs brew rescue.
        The cycle of the yardstick scraps the wand.
        The schoolma'ams rap the knuckles of the goddess
        And rout the gab and gape of song and shrine.
        White coats with questionnaires will sanitize her
        The way semantics fixed her bards up: language
        Homogenized and love depilatoried.

No god, no evil, no almost anything
Except the processed everything we'll vend you.

[*With triumphant bearing, aunts leave stage to go to bed. But
the instant they're gone, stage goes dim; lighting-effects shimmer
across ceiling.*]

WE: The other impersonations weren't like this one.
In her an uncontrollable unfolding;
In us a shriller giggle, sweating with frolic.
Sea-winds from out of bounds are taking over.
Suddenly air
Drags dense.
Far shell's
Long moan.
Taut
Room. Expectancy almost
Of miracle. O no, of hoax! Help, aunts!
An orgy of what must be sleights of hand
Spins round us in the very worst of taste:
Invisible dove-wings jumble up the ledger;
Our deadwood desks grow buds embarrassingly
Purple. It's she—quick, pelt her with bouquets
Of custard—let's all storm the stage together.
[*Invisible plastic barrier, descending, halts our storming of stage
and bounces custard pies back on ourselves.*]
We can't; she blurs, she blurs; the showgirl blurs
Into an Other; no clue except faint salt-spray;
The past we pelt compels us like morphine.
[*to dryad:*]
Your show's a flop. Get down. We're shaky; you
Are shiny with a voice above your voice.

[*Aphrodite voice now no longer comes from dryad's lips but from
spotlighted empty air at ceiling; meanwhile both dryad and we
face upward, rigid with stylized terror as if paralyzed by venge-
ful descent of some real deity.*]

APHRODITE VOICE [*above*]:
You poked apart the sleepwalk poise of things.
Your own sleep now
                 won't seal you from our waking.
God? No, but gods!—who'd strip for mere abstract ones?
Obscenely shrine, piously desecrate us,
Our swelling fruit half terror half decorum,
Flesh flushed with spilling wine: we touchable gods.
    . . . I still am I, the mussed-up goddess,
    Starlight and pond-scum tangled in a ditch.
    What I've arrived to bring, is not salvation—
    Too much of that too loud too many eons—
    But choice between two fires: love's and arson's;
    And each one pulsing, pulsing through all shields.
    Lively is not alive; a funeral pyre
    Is snugger than a hearth a little while.
Here comes a cypress jury-grove to judge
Your backtalk to the southwind. You have made,
By your definings and unsorceries,
The fig cloacal and the fountain chemic,
Whereby a sky's whole constellation crashed.
For this the Courts of Eros sentence you
To health,
          and to drum-majorettes,
                    and to
Your nightly screaming when my pulse throbs through.

[*Aunts rush out to the rescue, in nightgowns and with streaming
hair, and bang down the vaudeville curtain; the dimmed lights
flash once, like lightning, and die. Our closing speech is shouted
to each other in total dark.*]

WE: We've never felt so blind. Short circuit. Who did it?
The shining did it. What shining?
It's vanished from her. It couldn't—no clue except a
Faint fishy stench—have ever been really there.

ACT III

Scene 7, PANIC IN ARCADY

[*Left backdrop: tidy business office. Right: thicket labeled "AR-CADY." We enter out of breath and plead with dryad.*]

WE: We're on the lam from aunts
                    and from six lost maneuvers.
Inveigle from your slummy halfgod contacts
A hide-out for us in the land of Id.
What's going on beyond the schoolhouse hedges?
Fix us with some delirious new spasm
Out there among those reeds and all those pipings.
Here
[*gesturing at business office*]
      every racy action comes vicarious;
High jinks are as atrophied as the word "thus";
Everything's organized, and "thus" a bore.

SHE: Too late. You're filed in your own filing-system
With frayed manila-folders for your souls—
Once labeled "GOD'S OWN IMAGE: USE WITH CARE"
But now reclassified as "OBSOLETE."

WE: Serve us Arcadia, bodily and direct.
Brew us a witch-brew to outjump our skins,
To live on fresher levels even if brute ones,
As once delicious panic did where Pan was.

SHE: Passionate in Arcady? For once unvicarious?
Why, of course. I, illusionist, herb-brewer,
Reach you this jug of ironies. A gulp is your springboard.

[*We drink from her jug and bound from business backdrop to Arcady backdrop. During our long hallucinated speech that follows, nothing we describe—orgy, trampling, or Pan—is really there, except for a single ordinary goat.*]

WE [*to each other*]:
We've jumped to Arcady like champagned corks. Action
Thrums us like tics. We feel unleashed. We feel
Nature and naked freedom everywhere.
[*staggering violently, dazedly*]
Is it lava or waterfalls? . . . in either case
Shagginess comes at us. All over us. O and now
The goats themselves, cartoons of our own dawn.
But toothier. Bucking. The air steamy with wishes.
Look!—hooves are trampling the nipples of gross breasts;
The stare of noon winks its indulgence; we'll join them,
Rearing our shin bones, gymnasts of orgy,
Slobbering with surrealist derring-do.
      [*we rough-house with office furniture:*]
      Bellowing and walloping up and down verandas,
      Past widened eyes of courtiers and aghast cats,
      We throw chairs at each other; the air is splintry with
                                    wood;—
      [*seeing one small crow:*]
      Storms of black snowflakes caw into our ears.
[*Eerie pipings off-stage.*]
From goats that gods in heat have rubbed against,
From noon-mad thickets horned with shaggy hints,
An ancientness of winds in reed-pipes pities us:—

UNSEEN PAN VOICE [*from direction of goat and thicket*]:
Gardening their wishes, terrace over terrace,
My vineyard children knew: what counts is levels.
Your lusts are outburst, and you call them nature;
But on what level and with what a snigger!
Poison for you: the wines without the wine-god,

Our naked freedom without our measured dance.
Better than you: even my desert Foeman
And all His disproportion of sky to loam.
Better that drouth than hydroponic passions.
Sweeter that death than automats of life.

[*We bound back to right stage, in "panic."*]

WE: Goodbye to Arcady; Pan scared us so we
Jumped all the way home,
                              to this day reeking of goat.
. . . Trance. Jug. What did you do to us, witch?

SHE [*matter-of-fact voice*]:
The brew was water. The rest you supplied yourselves.

Scene 8, THE CASE FOR THE AUNTS

[*Yard outside garage. First they alone, then we alone. Dryad never appears in this scene, but throughout they and we glance nervously at closed garage door as if hearing unheard threshings behind it.*]

1st AUNT: Not with demure dropt eye but open bird-stare,
Her scorn shuts off the epoch she outfaces;
The nictitating membrane of her "no"
Falls with finality of sheet on corpse.

[*air of musing on past:*]
By all our outstretched shelter undiverted,
She clenched her course to her September purpose,
Torrential as a flock of redwinged blackbirds
Hurtling their gaudy wedge mile after mile
Southward through upward smoke of northern homes.

2nd AUNT: "Southward." The word warns of the middle sea,
Of gnat stings and production shortages,
Fume of siroccos, oils, and armpit shirt-stains.
Velvety sun-cubs, south of right and wrong,
Tan's irresponsibles, how they enrage us!
[*pitches monkey-wrench against tree.*]

3d AUNT [*grandiloquent voice, climbing step-ladder*]:
Along production-curves through doilied Edens,
All barbecue and plug-in Arcady,
86

The epoch's yes against the outlaw's no
Grates with diamond-hard complacency.
[*runs down ladder and kicks garage door.*]

2nd AUNT: So, at town brook, long day on day like this:
The sunrise sheens the rainfall on the water
So yellow that the splash-globes hang—raw berries—
Upon the stems of rays; hang, bob, and hang;
Then dusk; rays grope and miss; tarred bronze sags down.
Day after day. Who'll first erode? She, bribe-gashed?
They?
[*pointing at entering "we"*]
             —weak hard diamonds, gashed by their own dust.

[*Aunts leave while we wheel in big electronic brain, labeled "DEL-
PHIC COMPUTER."*]

WE [*bowed heads*]:
Delphic computer with thy brain of coils
To whom we stammer tremulous petitions,
Accept our offering of motor oils
And deign to grant us rub-off from omniscience.

[*By pouring libation from oil-can into slot, we activate the prose-
talking fact-machine. Its first two speeches are impersonal metal
voice; its third speech changes by stages, as if infiltrated, into warm
dryad voice.*]

DELPHIC COMPUTER:
If Croesus attacks the Persians, he will destroy a mighty empire.

WE: No, no, the question is:
[*half-glancing at garage*]   do gods exist?

COMPUTER:
The question is: is existence godlike?

WE: So much the worse for gods if they don't exist.

COMPUTER:
If they don't exist, so much the worse for existence.
Gods don't need existence;
For years they've managed nicely without it.
But existence needs *them;*
Existence without gods is birth without creation,
A museum where it is the living who are the mummies.

WE-SPOKESMAN [*to rest of us after reflective pause*]:
Wheel it away to the junk yard;
The coils got jinxed by throbs from the garage.

[*We leave right-stage, angrily dismantling computer. Aunts re-enter left-stage.*]

1st AUNT: Eroding us with glacier-slow retreats,
Those Old Expelled, and she their new return.

2nd AUNT: She doesn't recognize us (that's our trump)
Gum-shoeing through history as genial philistines,
Masking our hate, our beautiful hate, as progress.
Not aunts but deadpan pantomimes of aunthood:
[*scornfully adjusting our Hokinson-cartoon hats and gloves*]
What a humiliating masquerade!

1st AUNT [*voice curt, sober, dominant*]:
Endure it. There's a cause we're here for: justice.
We three against Aphrodite and her dryad;
A family feud between two factions of sisters;
Blood-born or foam-born, justice or love,
Both factions born from sky and both as queens.

3d AUNT [*over-eloquently, with fist-shakings at garage, embarrassing other two by such melodrama*]:
We recognize her all right, though she not us;
Love's spy, our lawless sister; oh those bitches!

1st AUNT [*calming her*]:
Yes, but fight by the code
Agreed on in the old days.
Remember the Concordat,
Remember the game-rules.

3d AUNT: Rehearse the strategy
For playing the game called "man."

1st AUNT: First coddle man; then

ALL: —sting.

1st AUNT: Sting man to get at *her*.

3d AUNT: To get at Sister Dryad?

1st AUNT [*impatiently*]:
To get, *through* her, at Sister Aphrodite.

[*Hearing our approach, aunts hastily arrange, as backdrop, a painting of tractor, ice cream cone, and drive-in church.*]

WE [*entering excitedly*]:
Outrage after outrage;
Pan after Aphrodite.
Even computers fail us.
Only you don't fail us.

THEY: After the vaudeville of the gods, we saved you
By yanking down the curtain just in time.

WE: After the Pan fiasco,
We saw how right you were
And spanked her merrily
And plunked her down upon her straw again.
How we depend on you!
Obeying you is freedom.

THEY: Freedom is luscious,
[*touching ice cream with classroom pointer, like kept scientist in TV commercial*]
                              and it ought to be.
Dynamic [*touching tractor*]
          and yet pain-relieving too. [*touching church*]

[*Aunts unfold three cots for us, seat us on them, and drowse us with hypnotic hands.*]

THEY: Now take your naps
[*we stretch out instantly*]
                              while we do practice-teaching
On dolls—now isn't that a lovely quaintness?—
Who we pretend are you,
[*noting we are asleep and cannot hear:*]
Ye verray parfit gentil sniveling knights.

[*Aunts trample down tractor-church backdrop. Revealed behind it are enormous cacti, from which hang shredded fineries, skeletons, and three impaled doll-replicas of "we," in boyscout shorts and business jackets.*]

1st AUNT: Justice is torture, and it ought to be.
Ice cream and smiles, of course, are what we stand for.
Except when torture has been justly earned.

2nd AUNT: And somehow, when we've thought enough about
              it,
It's always earned. We take our hats off to you

[*doffing hats to dolls in exaggerated deference*]
And give you what you merit,
[*removing hat-pins from hats*]
                              just like this!
[*They stab doll-replicas; we jerk uneasily but remain asleep.*]

3d AUNT [*to the sleepers*]:
And if our latest project to impale you
Parades in current mild-eyed civic virtues,
(Doom frocked in P.T.A. proprieties),
Why, that's the gag from which we maiden-dragons
Get—to use teen-age nouns—our charge, our kicks.
[*Exit 3d aunt.*]

2nd AUNT: Our righteous kicks. Don't blame us when the ar-
                    row
Your hybris launched becomes the thorn that lames you.
"People get what's coming to them," meaning:
What's coming *from* them. On this we rest our case.

[*Exit 2nd aunt. 1st aunt speaks "THE CACTI ODE" that follows. In line one at the word "their," she points to the cacti; in
line two at the word "you," she points to the theater audience;
at the words "gash," "ouch," and "reverse Sebastian," she gives
cacti thorns an affectionate familiar pat.*]

Their health is parch. Their moral code is gash.
          Root-anchored only when you watch them,
They hop and clown behind you when you don't.
          Older than sex, they grow by budding,
Oval on oval twigged of pulpier green.
          A continuity of lobsters,
A felininity of ambushers,—
          Saharas crammed into a crouch.
Who will solve this charade of the cactus menagerie,
          This earned ouch of the heel of strut,
Who but hate's tenderness, the Eros of torture,

The mutuality of wounds?
Here grows a target where the barbs land facing
    Outward,—a reverse Sebastian,
A retribution of boomerang porcupines.
    Then teach, didactic vegetable,
How justly man is aimed at by his aims,
    How in the archeries of ego
A target is a mirror is a scales.

Scene 9, OUR OWN FREE CHOICE

[*Outside, next to garage and tree.*]

WE: News!

THEY: Condense it.

WE: Mind boils down to numbers.
To figure hers, we've been experimenting.
As heralds of the dignity of man,
We raced her through a maze against a rat
And spun her in an orbit with an ape.
Yet she still keeps failing mechanical-aptitude tests.

THEY: God-aptitude—her immortality quotient—
Is the one trait there is no test for.

WE: And so no place for. Best to shoot at sight.
[*hesitantly, after pause:*]
But gods don't die.

THEY: Let old age do the weeding.

WE: But gods refuse to age.

THEY: Then fray her down.
Keep proving to her dryads can't exist.

WE: She keeps refusing to be non-existent.
Haunts trees but, once hacked loose, can not crawl back.

THEY: Complains but won't walk out while you've the feed-
        bag.

Axed from her own world, needs your economics.
Stick to the formula: she needs, you give, she changes.

WE: Won't change. Not jailed. And yet won't fly the coop.

[*Enter dryad; sits down, twined between tree roots; touches lyre hanging on branch to accompany her song that follows.*]

SHE:
What keeps me from flying? My roots have kept me from falling
All winter. When storm was pushing all winter,
And hunger pulled, and the ice, they kept me from falling.
Now feathers. New green ones. What keeps me from flying
When wood, at first sprout, is all set to wing off and touch sun?
Now when wings choose to be earth-anchored leaves
—(Always too much I've loved you, earth, always too much)—
The roots that kept me from falling keep me from flying.

WE: You've long enough loafed on the straw we pay for;
Tossing though you've no grief from us to toss for;
Bashing a whole foundation you should build for.

THEY: Shop for Right Attitudes and you'll be begged for:
Play charm consultant to an ulcer expert;
Meet his commuter-special with station wagon;
Park half a sec at Amor's supermarket
For vaseline and douche bag—'omnia vincit'
Means get-yourself-laid-by-Success-you-unwashed-wop.

SHE: How lays Success? Inside each gym of sphincters,
A cheated artist shrugs. Not Miss Hygeia's
Dart games, or quoits, assuage that artist watcher;
He stalks, through nerves, a fire that's more than nerve-ends,
The way a spark is through—and more than—rays.
Frisky Hygeia?—no! Then for that watcher
Maria's star?

No ray but earth's for him,—
Not even the tug-past-death of Mary's eyes,
Twice beautiful, with birth and then with heartbreak,
Standing there twice with Burden in her arms.
And yet, her eyes! No star but hers makes demos,
Grimy with push and honk, sigh shiningly
An instant
           when revering shudder bends
Even egalitaria's bumptious knees.
Half with regret, that watcher turns away
From desert's gallantest retort to grape.

WE: Not this, not that; not hygiene, not pure spirit;
Then tell us,
           whose the breast to ease the breast?

SHE: Not glut, not geld the carnivore; attune.
Face, face and clasp ferocious radiant chaos
Warm into Form, Ionia's molten dance.
        Am sent to hint this to the half-conditioned,
        Not you, the guardian aunts, but you the guarded;
        Sent vainly, but warmth cannot help speak out.
Then whose the breast? The name, the saving word is—

THEY: Whose breast indeed? Don't name it, or you'll conjure
A trail of seaweed here a second time.

WE: What's in a name?

THEY: Incendiary perfume!
One whiff—ask Troy—between two flippant nipples
Burns topless skyscrapers down. With grouchy bottoms
Your three squat aunts are here to squash that spark.

SHE: Omnia vincit anyhow.

WE: What's that?

THEY: You model boys, that's foam-child propaganda.
The juvenile delinquent of Olympos
Might kick you in the groin. So social conscience
Says, "Kick her first, the cops are on your side."
> [*turning to dryad*]
> And, little godling, as for you, don't gate-crash
> With peddling your "advice to lovelorn" column.
> Our fellows mail no dark nights of the soul
> Signed "Deeply Troubled"; they trust Auntie, thank
>> you,

> And need no butt-in tit to blubber on.

WE: Glibness is all. And you're its engineers
So wonderfully, you wonderful three, we wonder—
When we don't sleep well—who you really are.

THEY [*to each other*]:
Drop the tough line, sound the vox humana.
> [*to us*]
> We are man's forward push. We stand before you,
> All schoolma'am and all aproned earnestness,
> To dish the fudge of endless uplift out.
[*running across to give us maternal squeeze*]
Then take these hands; no, clasp them close; together
We'll window-shop time's most advanced bazaar.
Today calls out (yes crude still, yes unarty
But that which works, your one reality)
For you to trust it. Trust the sudden tender
Voice-break of us who scold you but to shield you.
And trust today's gods: scientific laws.
> The rest are ghosts. "The classics"?—no, let ghouls
> Go wading for those soggy olive-crowns
> Through dead Aegean backwash of the past.
> What's left of Aphrodite's thousand years?
> A slosh of gumboots round a garbaged urn.

SHE: I ghost, more fleshed than what today is living,
Have heard you
               (where?)
                       before. Same lofty pathos,
Disguising hate-of-love as love-of laws.

THEY: Even the sun won't overstep his measures
Or we handmaids of the law will find him out.

SHE: The same clawed hands, now antiseptic scalpels,
Moderned for moderns. Same selfrighteous envy
Of two elusives: mystery and dawdling.
Now by my tighter scalp I recognize you:
How you have changed, since last we met in Greece,
To chicken-pattied club queen, you Allekto;
You to dynamic fem-exec, Megaira;
And you, my snake-haired sister,
[jerks hat from 3d aunt's wriggly curls]
To dowdy-hatted Doc Tisiphone.
        [to us with air of hysteria]
        Furies and Aphrodite—war of sisters—
        The oldest war—the war for man—
        And I, love's sister and theirs—the endless choosing.
        Now your choice, too—between two fires.
        The wrong choice snugger—for a while. .
        [jerks aunt-glove]
        Scalpels, I tell you—claws—no hands at all.
        Saviors are loose, drop everything, run for your souls.

[Aunts pull free from her with air of dignified innocence and re
store concealing hats and gloves.]

THEY: What is an Allekto? Who heard of things like Megaira?
Meaningless names. An informer, baiting progressives.
A hysteric, showing poorly-controlled hostilities.
In short, a witch-hunter.

[*At trigger-word "witch-hunter," we shrink from her physically as from leper.*]
                   Put her on trial for slander.

WE [*sincere shocked voice*]:
An informer! Spitting
On home and mother.
We're hunting you,
You witch,
For starting witch-hunts.
Set up the court.
[*quickly dragging in benches and judgment seat*]
No court-room rules;
All shout at once;
Then we'll decide.
Who best serves man—that's us—will get our vote.

[*Aunts and dryad, sitting on opposite benches, from now on rise alternately to address our judges' rostrum. Via reversible stage-equipment of headgear and handgear, aunts from now on look like snake-haired clawing Furies whenever facing her but look like beaming helpmeets whenever facing us, both roles staged as equally "real." Masks on sticks may be alternated instead.*]

THEY: The joy of serving is its own reward;
We ask but this: to let us hand you heaven.
Plus this:
                   tool all reflection into reflex.
[*Their long hands dangle ambiguously.*]
These hands (who'd grudge a clawlet here and there)
Hand man the very sun as power-socket.

SHE: I see
          the claws of costumed hell exposed.

WE: We see
   nothing; only chic long gloves.
[*Thunder overhead; all look toward sky.*]

SHE: I hear
   the heavens roar at blasphemy.

WE: We hear
   nothing; only our jet-fleet's usual thunder.

SHE: One sees what one can. Reality has levels.

WE: One sees what one wills. We fact, you trance. Two
                                         rhythms.

SHE: One sees what one must.

WE: . . . Two rhythms bumped when
A fluke of ax un-treed a chink of dusk.
And all this came
[*throwing up hands, bewildered*]
               from just an hour's outing.

THEY: Curse that hour, curse it!—toothless traps
Bite deepest; curse the trail that bagged as trophy
A god pelt,
         cloaking some unsated tree-core,
A girl pelt,
         cloaking some carnivorous gap.

WE: Dear aunts, why so obsessed, dear maiden aunts,
With warnings against trapdoors? Were even you
Sixteen once? Sixteen in vain? You warn—we answer,
"Carnivorous but cute." A vulgar answer?

THEY: Not vulgar; shrill. Rat-squeak of the trapped male.

WE: Not shrill; provocative. To stir what moves you.
As judges, we probe motives even of saviors.

SHE: Hell hath no woman like a Fury scorned.

THEY: Romance remains half fiction and half friction;
As broad-viewed nurses, we endorse for you
The act, the health-need; not the love, the lie.
> [*shrieking:*]
> There is one enemy only; love is it;
> Meeting it, sting to kill; where dearest, deepest.
> [*rump and belly squirming with dirty excitement,*
> *bent double like egg-laying vermin:*]
> O to be born like wasps in caterpillars;
> Gaily, instead of love, to torture grubs.

[*sedater voice, regaining control:*]
Have they told you of a plant named "Venus fly-trap"?
That's what we save from.

WE: Beauty versus duty?

THEY: Subtler than that. Not duty but civic duty.

SHE: Spoken by hive-queens. Civic pap for hives.
I am a woman, I starve on duty.

THEY: For the first time in history enough bread for all.

SHE: Humanitarian wasps.
Novocaine before the sting.
> [*running up to our rostrum; urgent voice*]
> Reject me, and they're *in* you.
> They'll vanish. But in *you*.

THEY: Bumper crops so jumbo they'll break earth's back.
Paradise rammed down throats like the water-cure.

SHE: When you're the tech-tech-slob-kings of the world,
Production athletes with built-in Furies,
Ask yourself where THEY vanished to, and ponder
The grub with the egg in him. A clue: your hearts
[insolently scratching our chests]
Will itch you then with a deep dryness.
And once inside you, they'll re-edit you;
They'll eat your memory, and you'll forget.

THEY [pushing her away from our hearts]:
Envy from exiled ember.

SHE: My rhythm warms the dance.
Theirs is the second flame.
It heats but cannot warm.
It stuffs your cities fat.
Then hangs them upside-down,
Gutted—bleeding red-hot slag.

THEY [to us]:
We get a bad press from love's agitator
[pointing at dryad]
Because our bloodhounds nip her. But to you
[ingratiating bow]
Our civic hounds, between their fangs, deliver
Official happiness like a gazette.

WE [to her]:
Their highest bid. Now what can you deliver?

SHE: Only this echo from an undertow:
>   To the doomed the wrong choice first feels right; a
>   pyre
>   Feels snugger than a hearth a little while.
Hail man-the-improver,
For his is the end of the world. In Technicolor.

WE: We were only taking a walk.
We were only leveling a gnarl.
We didn't ask to overhear eons wrangling.
We didn't intend to commit history.
Why must we choose?

[*We bolt for exit, but aunts and dryad both force us back into our judgment seats.*]

SHE: A fluke of ax has made you final judges
Between two armies: line and cycle, deadlocked
Since the first campfire split into two flames.

THEY [*to her*]:
The war has rules. Remember the Concordat.
The higher the stakes, the more precise the ritual.

WE: Why are *we* needed?

SHE: By the Concordat,
I cannot stop them direct, only through you.

THEY: We cannot stop her direct, only through you.

SHE: They and I are immortal, we do not exist.
Except through you.

THEY: Except through your free choice.

[*She and they throw themselves on knees before us, at our judges'
rostrum, and continue to address not each other but us.*]

SHE: We are your inside shadows—

THEY: As you are ours.

SHE: Man will become what you choose—

THEY: The stakes are man.

SHE: Circle or line. Choose.

THEY: She or we. Choose.

SHE: In you the war.

THEY: From you the future.

SHE and THEY: Choose!

WE: Whether to skim a shard on timeless waters
Or pant ahead in vertigo's contraptions?
Condone or prod the slow unfold of things?
Two passwords to unlock the code of things:
Listen to each leaf grow its own faint cycle—
Or shout it down with ax, unheard of power.
          [*banging gavel*]
          We choose the second, choose the aunts as future.
          The line, the line!—no matter where it leads.

[*We put dog collar around her neck and hand the slack leash to
aunts. At the word "neck" below, they jerk it strangle-tight, as
curtain falls on scene 9.*]

THEY: Our leveling down of global gnarls redoubles;
Reels the same celluloid from kraal to igloo;
De-animates the cosmos to a cakemix,
As standard as the fetlocks of a jeep.
O that men's gods had but a single neck,
To beefburg in the same disposal-grinder!

Scene 10, WE RAN ALL THE WAY HOME

[*Garage floor; now with human-size bird cage * over her and straw. At first, she and cage are veiled from view by side-curtain, while we address each other through alternating spokesman.*]

WE-SPOKESMAN:
The disturber
[*pointing at label* "DRYAD CAGE" *on side-curtain*]
          —remember her famous trial
For witch-hunt slanders against aunts and blueprints?
Bars ought to bar things, but there's mischief still;—

WE: Delicate music we thought we had forgotten,
Delicate music, fierce because forgotten,
Unnerves us with the implicating laughter
Of delicate music when we most forget her.
      So inland windows stare our thirst out after
      White sails, our own by birth but best forgotten.

WE-SP.: That's why we twitch so nervously at noise;
At every luncheonette her pulse has spies,—

WE: Game-keepers of the non-existent gods.
With all our merit-badges on,
We skulk like poachers to our Seat of Honor.

WE-SP.: Its creaky springs snort "no!" beneath our worldly
        weight.
"Garçon," we say, "that's *her* laugh. Throw her out."
He says, "What laugh, sir?"

---

* When staging, use same cage as in aunt partition in scene 5.

WE: Then we know it's us.

WE-SP.: Only it isn't. To prove it isn't, we judges
Sentenced her not to jail and not to madhouse
But to this cage
[*kicks it*]   (call it true liberty)
For inmates till they freely share our "yes."

WE: Till *she* stops tickling other people's sleep.

WE-SP.: But still she slips away.

WE: From this firm cage?

WE-SP.: Of course not. Inward. In—well, into shaping.

WE: What does she shape?

WE-SP.:   Herself. Each mood a tree,
Gesticulating with her entire flesh
Through that green gamut of her wreath of smocks,
Benignly elmed, aethereally aspened,
A menacing kaleidoscope of tendrils.
At last with one last leafy lilt of shoulders
She shudders to a halt, still flushed with trance,
Yet poised like oak. And speaks some oak-like curse—

SHE [*unseen, from within curtained cage*]:
            Impiety of fungus against root.
            Impertinence of number against seed.
            Merely the fact that you're so many of you
            Is smirk for incest, treason, plague to heal.

WE-SP.: You hear? She still won't stop it though we drugged
        her.

WE: We hiked to her garage dorm, spruced it up with
Bars into really not too glum a cell.
"To help you help yourself to be mature,"
That's what was pledged her; "for daft wings a cage."

WE-SP.: Chain stopt much nonsense; only her locks now
                threshing,—
Fever of clouds across her forehead's moon.

WE: That orbitless sick moon our purging kindness
Drains glow-worm dim.

WE-SP.:   A sneaky ember silvers
Outrageously between the bars of norm,—
Whenever, chained or bribed, she still says "no."
You'll hear her; even if gagged, she'd say it still,
The one vile puking way still left to say it.

SHE [*unseen*]:
At hefty orbit sleazily genteeled
        (Shuttling from chintzy homes to brassy markets,
        From tactful tantrums of your filtered hearts
        To drive-in heavens of a public grin)
My unchromed gullet vomits, vomits, vomits.

[*We jerk side-curtain from cage, reveal her threshing about.*]

WE: Just hear that vileness of last gasp of gods!
Yet that foul no, the same that threshed our sleep through,
Somehow rejoices more than all our yes.
Rejoicing oceanic resonances—
Dolphins of air—tinkle her chains like gauds.
Far off, where bulging breakers shriek their spray
Of birthday round a trouble-making island,
Her pulse finds girl communion.
[*she stands up, her back to us*]

Drawing up from
The caterwauling deeps at Kýthera
That pain-surviving bitch-tenacity
That just can't help enduring through and through,
She prays her final prayer. But this time peer to peer,
Tree-skirt to foam-skirt sister, tide to tide.

[*We contemptuously let her out of cage for final prayer to
Aphrodite.*]

SHE: Undertow,
You other blue,
Tow these to you.
Came sky; in upside-down of sky, there always
Was undertow.

WE: You are alone. Silence below.

SHE: Came Greek year; shrines held only what a port can
Of undertow.

WE: Silence below.

SHE: Came eons, Lilith, Venusberg; there always
Was undertow.

WE: Silence below.

SHE: Queened, demoned, pseudo-tamed, renamed, there al-
      ways
Was undertow.
Lines of the straighteners, net of nerves and subways,
Came; always indestructible below
Is undertow.

WE: Silence below.

SHE: Now undertow's
Fierce coarseness, sinew us who are so birch-bark
Gentle we pale with gladness at glint of dew.
Them, goddess, too,
Swerve
       not too late
              from where they hurtle to;
Sway up unearned—for these who earn the lightning—
The olive too.

WE: You are alone. Those prayed to, cannot hear you.
Those prayed for, we ourselves, don't need your prayer.

SHE: Once holy dread came

WE: —it was faulty light bulbs—

SHE: Tangy with clues of sea

WE: —on a rigged stage.
Here is no stage, no shrine; here is reality,
Gothic with gargoyles but not frilled with gods.
No salt-wind speeds here this time. Silence below.

SHE [*looking past us*]:
Then, under-goddess, must they all the way
(From whiz to slag) plumb their own plumb-line's end?
       Once there were promises intense as noons;
       It would have been a planet fit for lovers;
       There is dew on certain lanes on certain mornings
       That's neither air nor pool but waiting shyness.
       There's haze—faint red more white than any white
                               is—
       Haze that takes off at the first hint of sunrise
       Like a flamingo startled by a gun.

They tried to force the wooed consent of things.
A sea swayed up a choice between two fires.
O pity them, I smell the ashes in the skull.*
                    [*hands gentle on our shoulders, voice of compassion*]
          No helping you. The choice, the core is gone.
          No green except from arson's further shore.

WE: How caged and how unreachable she stands there,
How royal-slim within imagined pine!

SHE: Nears its end the chummy phase of will, male, steel,—
Bang triply stoked. A few toys more, then feeds
Your ash my wilds,
                    re-greened,
                              —wild sap, strict dance:
The second bloomtide of the hacked first gods.

[*Lights out and curtain falls.*]

          .   .   .

[*Lights. Placard:* "EPILOGUE, TEN YEARS LATER
                    = PROLOGUE RESUMED
                    WITH IN-BETWEEN FORGOTTEN."
*In front of unraised curtain we resume—as if amnesiac—same situa-
tion (same postures, same reminiscing-about-dryad) as in our PRO-
LOGUE of scene 1 before interrupted by the now vanished and
forgotten aunts. Difference is we now look ten years older: gray-
haired Elder Statesmen above waist, but still boy-shorts below.*]

---

  * For stage version only: on screen behind our triumphant faces and
seen only by audience, there flames up a colored slide-projection of the
famous mushroom cloud (as per scene 9 on "the end of the world in
Technicolor"). After "then feeds your ash my wilds," screen changes to
future groves blooming from cinders.

WE: Last visit there let's kiddingly recall.
The waif we pay. Or pay for, that she's cared for.
Dazed like some animal poisoned by practical jokers,
She suddenly looking laughably broken, a zoo.
       (Then why not looking older? One more puzzle:
       Was there always only us, or others, others?
       Our itching hearts forget; it was years ago.)
Trailed flowers once. Trails end on bestial floor.
In contrast, how we've prospered!—full of life
[quite unconsciously scratching our chests]
Like chubby grubs that burst with health and laugh at roses.
       (She said things; we had sense, we stuffed our ears.)
Ever since the year the others vanished
We boss unheard of power, tame as flame.
And what with Such Responsibilities
No time for visits. Only this last quick one—

[Curtain rises behind us and shows her sprawling full-length on
garage floor like degraded beast. Our voice and manner: strained
cheeriness, revulsion barely mastered by clinical detachment.]

WE: So many years since then, so fast so useful,
We thought we had forgot you. But we're back.
Just casually back.
[She rustles on straw, ignores us.]
Messy the end. Yet uncontrollable still;
Tainted with spontaneity to the last.
Same gracious straw, and same tune-fingered tossing
That fumbled at us once like witch at cradle.
But now so weak a twitch (though never stopping)—

SHE [without getting up or looking up]:
The wrong one snugger for a little while.

WE: —so weak a twitch, as good as stopt already.
These days we work so hard we just don't notice

Sub-tunes. Look up, we've brought you candied fruit.
[*louder, voice breaking:*]
Stop, stop it totally; filth, leave our sleep alone!

SHE [*painfully pulling herself up*]:
You nagged apart the flowing dark of things.
Was that your bliss, to mesh your flesh to gears?
Here's light to counterscorch enlighteners then.
I, struck down waking, strike you through your sleep with
One splinter from some palmy dream you felled
   (Of pulse the prancing or of sweat the sweetness,
   The answered press of nipples in the dark
   Or airy shyness of a morning traipse);
This one last life-shred not yet chilled by steel,
One tinder in your heart-wall's driest chink,
Will niche such arson there you'll howl aloud
The corpse-stink of the boredom of your bliss.

WE: Candy for inmates. We paid you. Well, what gift more?

SHE: One gift only: the tune you choke in you,
The tone, the tone—unfiltered—of private warmth.

WE [*turning our backs on her and facing audience head-on*]:
Last visit; voice, warmth, strangeness scared us so we
Ran all the way home though it was half a mile.

APPENDIX:

SHORT NARRATIVE VERSION

Publisher's Note: This is the original undramatized version that appeared in magazine form with *Poetry*, Chicago.

WE RAN ALL THE WAY HOME

1

Callously innocent in our disinfected games,
We plastic-swaddled children of fifty years
With unlined faces, hacking down some gnarls,
Unpeeled a dryad once, stript, trapt, and spitting,—
That older race, filth of unswaddled pulse-beat,
A god and shieldless,
                                    uninnocently tender.

2

Plodding back home, yanking a god we cornered:
A lassoed cataract amid canals.
Then hours of swapping new toys for old spells,
Till sobered by the hygiene-spraying aunts:
"What makes our young ones fuss round just some stump?
Go clutter honest lumber up with spooks,
Read dryads in, go hunt for haunters; yet
When all is said and done of 'myth' and 'magic',
One flashlight shrivels any hunk of dusk.
But watch for tricks: with lyric buzz re-enter
Flies, incense, backwardness, those Old Expelled.
Her spells?—her frauds! Aim lights—look, nothing there."

3

Frauds of the dryad:
                                    speech, growth, weapon mocked us.
Her weapon: raids by quicksilver evadings.
Her growth: tree rhythm, an unfolding. Her speech:
A riffraff of breezes, truant from asphalt and logic,
Leaving behind a litter of petals and doubts.

Of anti-metal something shimmered then
(A winging of sap against a steeling of will)
That would have rusted something of machine in us,
Had something in us of weight not tamed that wine.
We tamed by gifts. Gave metal's just-as-good:
"Instead! Instead! You need; we give; you change."
. . . And so a god gets nursed into a pet;

4

But threshes about.
                          Exchanged her splintry wood—
Imagine being cooped in living coarseness—
For kind soft straw we dumped upon the pavement
Of a prefab garage we lavished on her,
A half-mile from our street. Ingratitude
Of gods we house! Not one gift worked
To stop that twisting on that first-class straw.

5

A far-off tremor shook our sleep that evening;
A twirl of arms and boughs; recurrent dream:
No start
        Around around,
                She is a god she is a plant
                        Undertow of flesh and ocean
                        Ocean and flesh of undertow
                A plant is she a god is she
        Around around,
No end.

6

That obscene vibrance jarred our own snug beds
And blighted every crib from birth with pulse:
"Dear aunts, we have bad dreams, seal unrest out."
So much of other nuisance, junk, and murk
We've killed for its own good, to scrape earth pure;

But when some bitch-dog wags immortal hide,
Our "put her out of her misery" won't put.
A rotten gyp when gift and gun both fail;
No other vermin lasts; it's them, it's she, it's
Immortals always spoil our cleaning up.
. . . And so a pet gets cursed into a god.

7

Next dream, half farce; she sowed—amid tame starches—
Song's fleeing laurel, wriggly still with nymph,
And love's wild myrtle,—till a crop of sighs
Drowned out the crackle of our breakfast cornflakes.
        "Spry aunts, help quick; growth shrinks us; school in panic.
        Whatever sprouts, throbs to the dryad's tossing."
"Growth just won't shape like plastics, you poor boys;
To wither myrtle, plant it in a pot;
To wither laurel, spray it with a footnote.
But darker than her wars, her lures. Those fancy
God-molls got gossiped of in Arcady.
Neighbors saw them bend near bulls, and as for swans—.
Then stomp more moral than a quadruped;
Be well-scrubbed knights; in short, go lynch that foreigner."
. . . Creation gets reversed to kill a god.

8

What cannot kill unkillable, can torture;
She, writhing stubborn, droned unwelcome myth:
"*Two signs, when first your campfire banned us, wrangled:
Circle and line. Our cycle, your ascent.
'Revere each season's own true bend,' we sang then;
'Drain, build, stamp logic on,' clanged will, male, steel.
Clang-knit geometries of girders garland
Your plumb-lines now*
                    and grid our zigzag ways."

"Bulldozer world: grove's awe and rubble razed for
A smile of blueprints on a surge of chins."

"*Your lavishness with clicks and slot machines—*"

"*—(here tin gives birth, true stainless birth, not life's kind)—*"

"*—is but man's fear of liking being owned again
By cornucopian lap.*"
                    "All nest and trap and
Prayer lips and infinite pillowing mercy . . . and quicksand.
Hail man-the-improver, for his is the world without end."

From deicide, man deified. But she:

9

"*Girl was the older race's core, unshrined by
Who shrines machine, the heavy public man
Too willed to play or pray. And girlhood once
Uprooted roots out child, man, landmark too,
Untending—to be priestess means to tend—
The linking ivy of a heritage.
Apart, apart the mute shared sap-flow dries,
Into a crackle of unclutching. Hail
The chattery scorch-torch-ping of progress popping.*"

"Back to your lute-strings; our rustproof nerves twang prose."

"*What have you prosed us to?—once tide, ode, bud.
Good for your files and glands, the thing your time-clock
And cot call 'woman' means but gelded male.
Yet girl-lap templed—inner Delphi—teaches
        Doer what grower knows of spell and rite,
        Willing what being knows of soul and gut.*"

"A belly swelled into an oracle?"

"*Don't think apart the mixed-up dark of things.
As we need your half, starving you'll need ours;
No crop from conquering plow without our furrow;
Spray all your fruit-trees clean, they still won't dangle
Till fouled into life by dryad-rut within.*"

10

Our words were such as best reduce to numbers
And freeze apart the mixed-up flow of things.
Her words were how she joined them,—chunky crystals;
Meanings, not numb in maps but felt in facets,
Flecked them now fierce, now farcical, now wistful.
    We offered her distraction's mezzanine
    And of synthetics all the plush and chock-full:
    "You swigged our swill; then drink our team-pledge too."
    But threshed the more. An elbow-jarring cadence
    Jostled our jorum of prosperities:
    "What hoists mirage, can't push one jonquil up;
    Spore, shammed from sand, climbs facile,

                                    towers, keels."
Not with demure dropt eye but open bird-stare,
Her scorn shut off the epoch she outfaced;
The nictitating membrane of her "no"
Fell with finality of sheet on corpse.
By all our outstretched harvest undiverted,
She clenched her course to her September purpose,
As sagittal as flocks of redwinged blackbirds
Hurtling their gaudy wedge mile after mile
Southward through upward haze of outstretched grain.
    "Southward." The word warns of the middle sea,
    Of gnat stings and production shortages,
    Fume of siroccos, oils, and armpit shirt-stains.
    Velvety sun cubs, south of right and wrong,
    Tan's irresponsibles, how they enrage us!
    Along production-curves to neater Edens,
    All barbecue and plug-in Arcady.
    The epoch's yes against the outlaw's no
    Grated with diamond-hard complacency.
So, at town brook, long day on day like this:
The sunrise sheened the rainfall on the water
So yellow that the splash-globes hung—raw berries—
Upon the stems of rays; hung, bobbed, and hung;
Then dusk; rays groped and missed; tarred bronze bulged down.
Day after day. Who'd first erode? She: bribe-gashed.
We: weak hard diamonds gashed by our own dust.

11

Was heard to pray when thought herself unheard:
   "*You high ones, old ones, watching two by two*
   Wherever shrineless gods are exiled to,
   Send down your lightning. But your olive too.
   Cool whisper of the ages, not the age,
   Expand the shallows of men's anchorage,
   Apprentice them to more than they can hear.
   You earth-deep resonance they dare not hear,
   Be everywhere, like fragrance of the orange,
   Yet single and sonorous as its root,
   Till lives are sweet and inward as an orange,
   And every death a quilt of leaves on root."

12

Nerve-drugs for war words; for daft wings, a cage.
We hiked to her garage dorm, spruced it up with
Bars into really not too glum a cell:
"To help you help yourself to be mature."
Chain stopped much nonsense; only her locks now threshing,—
Fever of clouds across her forehead's moon.
That orbitless sick moon our purging kindness
Drained glow-worm dim; yet sneaky silver embered
Outrageously between the bars of norm—
Whenever, chained or bribed, she still said "no".
The one vile puking way still left to say it:
"*At hefty orbit sleazily genteeled*
      (*Shuttling from chintzy homes to brassy markets,*
      From tactful tantrums of your filtered hearts
      To drive-in heavens of a public grin)
   My unchromed gullet vomits, vomits, vomits."

13

Oh aunts, the vileness of last gasp of gods!
Yet that foul no, the same that threshed our sleep through,
Somehow exulted more than all our yes.

Exultant oceanic resonances—
Dolphins of air—tinkled her chains like gauds;
Far off, where bulging breakers shriek their spray
Of birthday round a trouble-making island,
Her pulse found girl-communion.
                              Drawing up from
The caterwauling deeps at Kýthera
That pain-surviving bitch-tenacity
That just can't help enduring through and through,
She prayed her second prayer. But this time peer to peer,
Tree-skirt to foam-skirt sister, tide to tide:—
"*Undertow,*
  You other blue,
  Tow these to you.
  Came sky; in upside-down of sky, there always
Was undertow.
  Came Greek year; shrines held only what a port can
Of undertow.
  Came eons, Lilith, Venusberg; there always
Was undertow.
  Queened, demoned, pseudo-tamed, renamed, there always
Was undertow.
  Lines of the straighteners, net of nerves and subways,
Came; always indestructible below
Is undertow.
  Now undertow's
Fierce coarseness, sinew us who are so birch-bark
Gentle we pale with gladness at glint of dew.
Them, goddess, too,
Swerve
       not too late
                    from where they hurtle to;
Sway up unearned for these who earn the lightning,
The olive too."

                              14

Silence below. Prayer scorned. "You are alone."
"*Silence? No balm for these but their own ghat?*

They tried to force the wooed consent of things.
Then, under-goddess, must they all the way
(From whiz to slag) plumb their own plumb-line's end?
Once there were promises intense as noons.
Hail man-the-improver,
For his is the end of the world. In technicolor."
      To us: "Lively is not alive; a pyre
      Seems snugger than a hearth a little while."
Then royal-slim within imagined pine:
"Nears its end the chummy phase of will, male, steel,—
Bang triply stoked; a few toys more, then feeds
Your ash my wilds,
              re-greened;
                         wild sap, strict dance;
The second bloomtide of the hacked first gods."

15

Last visit there let's kiddingly recall,
She suddenly looked laughably aging, a zoo.
Messy the end. Yet uncontrollable still
      (Same scene; that gracious straw; last twitch of tossing)
Tainted with spontaneity to the last:
"You nagged apart the flowing dark of things.
Was that your bliss, to mesh your flesh to gears?
Here's light to counterscorch enlighteners then.
I, struck down waking, strike you through your sleep with
One splinter from some palmy dream you felled
      (Of pulse the prancing or of sweat the sweetness,
      The answered press of nipples in the dark
      Or airy shyness of a morning traipse);
This one last life-shred not yet chilled by steel,
One tinder in your heart-wall's driest chink,
Will niche such arson there you'll howl aloud
The corpse-stink of the boredom of your bliss."

"Candy for inmates. We paid you. Well, what gift more?"

"One gift only: the tune you choke in you,
The tone, the tone—unfiltered—of private warmth."
Last visit; voice, warmth, strangeness scared us so we
Ran all the way home though it was half a mile.

CHANGES FOR ACTED VERSIONS

(made for the Cambridge performances, etc.)

Screen projections of slides may replace backdrops, placards, props. Two hardest acting problems for "we": (1) to convey in scenes 1–9 not only our obvious submission to aunts but also our repressed dryad-induced impulse toward freedom; (2) to convey in scene 10 and epilogue not only our official total triumph but also our unaware total defeat. To bring out both pairs of ambivalences for audiences unfamiliar with the book, add such emphases here and there as (for example) repeating twice our unconsciously ironic phrase "tame as flame" on p. 111 of epilogue, using a confident voice the first time, a hesitant voice the second time.

Cuts for more compact sense of movement (in acted versions only): omit everything between line 8, p. 29 and "Other freedom-talkers," p. 30; end scene 3 with "guilty face," p. 33; omit all scene 8 before "Eroding us," p. 88; cut first 8 lines of "Cacti Ode," p. 91; omit all scene 9 before "You've long enough," p. 94; omit all scene 10 before p. 107 except to retain "we judges" (p. 106, line 2) through "share our yes." To condense scenes 4, 5, 6, omit first two autumn songs, also "Line Against Circle," "Golden Banality," all Melpomene, first Athena speech, etc. To precede or half-way interrupt third autumn song of pp. 48–50, insert lines 10–13 ("I see" etc.) from deleted p. 36, further clarifying that song's 3-cornered fight by perhaps adding a short direct prose summary of each corner, freely adapted (into dialogue form) from pp. 12–13 of preface.

These and many other necessary differences from book version were separately copyrighted by author in 1960 with Library of Congress as a drama typescript and were included in 1961 in the Cambridge Poets' Theater script; for permission to use it, address author % Mt. Holyoke College, South Hadley, Mass.

Line 4 of page 69 steals from Sophocles; lines 19–20 of page 76 from Euripides; speech 2 of page 97 from Heraclitus. (In no case learnedly but via second-hand highschool cribs.) The aunts, speaking each above line, do so with source-concealment since their secret depends on concealing their familiarity with Greek. The concluding couplet of scene 9 ("O that men's gods had but a single neck, / To beefburg in the same disposal-grinder!") is meant to misquote Emperor Caligula's "utinam populus Romanus unam cervicem haberet!" Similarly the Akhilles reaction to drive-in churches on page 37 is merely a modernization of his comment in Book XI, lines 489–91 of the *Odyssey*. The prediction by the Delphic Computer, page 87, about the self-destructive war of Kroisos (Croesus), is quoted from Herodotos, *Histories*, Book I, chapter 53, section 3.

Hesiod's *Theogony*, lines 183–7, here partly paraphrased on page 45, makes sisters of Aphrodite, the Furies, and the *meliai*-nymphs. Our heroine (sown from the same wound of Ouranos as her sister-ally, Aphrodite, and love's enemies, the Furies) is a *melia*, not a *dryas*. But in English it comes more natural to use the more familiar word "dryad" broadly for both rather than confine her to any one species of tree. . . . The song of the muse Melpomene on page 71 is from Menon's lament for Diotima. That quotation is here translated for two contradictory reasons: first, to fill objective literary needs (the context calls for a quotation from the muse's purest singer—who else but Hoelderlin?); second, to fill mere private needs (translation as a libation of reverence for one's betters).